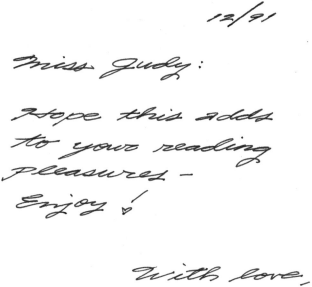

12/91

Miss Judy:

Hope this adds
to your reading
pleasures —
Enjoy!

With love,
Ms H.
XXX ooo

Books by Alice Kahn

Multiple Sarcasm
My Life as a Gal
Luncheon at the Cafe Ridiculous

Luncheon at the

CAFE

RIDICULOUS

Alice Kahn

POSEIDON PRESS

New York   London   Toronto   Sydney   Tokyo

Poseidon Press
Simon & Schuster Building
Rockefeller Center
1230 Avenue of the Americas
New York, New York 10020

Designed by Chris Welch
Manufactured in the United States of America
1 3 5 7 9 10 8 6 4 2
Library of Congress Cataloging-in-Publication Data
Kahn, Alice, date
Luncheon at the Cafe Ridiculous/Alice Kahn.
p.   cm.
1. United States—Social life and customs—1971–
2. United States—Social life and customs—1971–
—Humor.   I. Title.
E169.04.K34   1990
973.91—dc20   89-27388
CIP
ISBN 0-671-69150-3

Grateful acknowledgment is made to the following publica-
tions, in whose pages these articles first appeared:

Los Angeles Times Magazine: "Esalen at 25: The Legendary
Human-Potential Mecca Has Changed—But the Magic Remains," December 6, 1987.

Elle magazine: "Power Drinking," October 1987

(*continued on page* 287)

Thanks a lot...

Peter Sussman, Rosalie Wright,
Bill German, Lou Schwartz,
Don Michel, John Brownell,
Shelby Coffey, Ellen Levine, Ann Patty,
Eddie's brain, my friends (you know
who you are)
and every reader who wrote.

Contents

three: Channeling for Dollars 119

four: The Family That Shabooms Together 163

Luncheon at the Cafe Ridiculous

"I don't think I was meant to be a mother," Bree Wellington told her old friend Mai Blender over lunch at The Quilted Adobe.

"Meant, *schmeant*," opined Mai, a licensed therapist and an amateur sarcasticist. "You've got the kid. Even Nordstrom won't take her back."

"Of course, I love Rachel Whoopi as I've never loved another human being. I can't imagine life without her," said Bree, fiddling with the heel of the baguette. "It's just that I don't think I have the patience."

They were interrupted by the sight of the waiter standing there like a symphony conductor demanding their complete attention before he began his performance.

"Our specials today are the George Bush Squid Pro Quo with a confit of figs, papayas, mango and corn. We also have a Dan Quail, lightly roasted with a polenta happy face. And finally, there is the Jim Wright Pork Barrel with a salad of mixed greens and aged goat cheese. The soup today is chayote, and our wine of the week is Cheek Creek white zinfandel at six-fifty a glass."

"Do we get to keep the glass? Does it have our team's name on it?" asked Mai.

"I'll have the Bush and a glass of the Creek," said Bree, her look telling the waiter to indulge her boorish friend.

"Gimme the Quail and a glass of Diet Coke with a twist," Mai told the waiter. Then she turned to Bree and asked, "You paying?" After Bree nodded, Mai added, "Throw in a bowl of the chayote soup."

"Mommy, Mommy," screamed the little boy at the next banquette, "that lady's eating a coyote."

"Nicodemus," said his mother. "Get your bolo tie out of your spaetzle!"

Mai looked at the boy and then made the finger-down-the-throat gesture to Bree. She leaned forward and whispered, "Hell is other people's children."

She moved on to another subject that she knew would get a rise out of Bree. "Have you heard the latest about Neal Blender?" she asked, referring to her husband circa 1974 and Bree's lover circa 1984. "He's dating Cher," she said and began snickering.

"But that's impossible," Bree protested. "Neal's over thirty."

"I know," Mai cackled, "but it's true. He told me she might even name a perfume after him—Neal. But she'll spell it K-n-e-e-l. Kneel by Cher—share the fantasy—something like that."

"Forgive me, Mai. I know you were married to the man for five years, but why would anybody give up that pretty little Rob Camilletti for a balding, forty-year-old wannabe screenwriter?"

"I guess for the same reason that you almost broke up with Dirk to nestle with Neal."

"Now, just a minute. That was before Dirk and I were married and, of course, well after your separation from Neal."

"Relax," said Mai, picking up the crumbs of the baguette from the tablecloth and licking them off her fingers. "Neal and I had an open marriage anyway. That's why we ended up divorced."

Just then, the waiter put down the bowl of chayote and slid the squid toward Bree. As they were digging in, a man in a military uniform with a bandolier belt across his chest suddenly raced through the terra cotta restaurant brandishing a machine gun. A fig fell from Bree's mouth to the floor.

The man fired a rat-a-tat at the ceiling, but nothing happened. Then he shouted, "The crème brûlée is excellent!"

The waiters then surrounded him and escorted him out like assistants at a James Brown concert. Before he exited through the kitchen, he screamed back, "The crème brûlée—and tell them Gaucho sent you."

There were just ten seconds of silence before the sophisticated urban diners, accustomed to a world of mania and mayhem, returned to quiet talk about ruined relationships and done deals.

Mai slurped her chayote and said, "This restaurant-as-theater bit has gone too far."

one

The
VALLEY
of ART
PSYCHOSIS

Born with a
Silver Popcorn Box

I was born in a balcony at the Lawndale Theater on Roosevelt Road near Pulaski in Chicago. My daddy owned the picture show.

My mother told me that she used to leave me in my crib up in the balcony with a favorite usher, a man named Big Ben. Ben was six feet six and four hundred pounds with his shoes off. In between the double features, he'd take me out for a couple Romanian garlic steaks and several chocolate malts. What I couldn't eat, Big Ben would finish.

I was about four years old when I became conscious of this whole scene. The time was the late 1940s, and the popular films of the day were moody private detective stories—film noir—and screwball comedies. As a result, I came to think of life as a dark, menacing screwball comedy, a philosophy that has stood the test of time.

To my knowledge, no one has studied the psychological effects on a kid of continually watching forties movies and eating Milk Duds nonstop. We do read a lot about how a generation raised on television threatens our future. During the last election a survey of young book-club members—junior intellectuals—revealed that they believed Pee-wee Herman was as qualified for the presidency as Michael Dukakis. Which either proves that all short guys look alike or explains how George Bush came to be president.

I know that one result of my childhood was that I believed that time was an enormous clock whose hands could speed up or go backward, that the days of our lives were calendar pages flying in the wind and that space was a fast-moving train rolling through towns named Milford's Landing, Altoona, Cedar Rapids, and Laramie.

I thought that men wore big hats and greatcoats to hide their shoulder holsters. I thought that women wore cloche hats and carried leather bags containing pearl-handled revolvers. I thought every town but mine had a soda shop owned by a guy called Pops who slapped his face and said, "Sheesh!"

Mostly, I thought picture shows were palaces and that my dad was a king. When we walked down the street, everyone knew him and said hello. He was a man who brought them joy. He was the guy who introduced Screen-O (big-screen Bingo on Saturday nights). He was the killjoy who nabbed them sneaking in the exits.

One day, I was either sitting in the easy chair pretending I was Barbara Stanwyck fleeing a killer or I was standing in front of the mirror in high heels wondering how I'd ever grow up to be Betty Grable. My dad told me he was selling the theater. TV was coming in. Besides, his mother had just died, and he said he didn't "want to be around music anymore."

After that we'd spend a lot of time in other people's theaters. Mostly we'd go on sweltering summer days when those melting ice-cube letters spelling out "Air Conditioned!" beckoned like an oasis.

To my dad, it was strictly business. He'd comment on how empty the theater was, how low the grosses must be, how dirty the lobby looked, how the bulbs in the stars in the ceiling needed replacing and, finally, how lousy the cast was in the movie. As soon as the film came on, he'd fall asleep.

He was growing old. He was a deposed king stuck in someone else's empire. The Lawndale, his kingdom, had been sold. It was reopened after a Name-the-Theater contest as The Rena. They gave away free dishes to try to lure people in.

I'd watch him sleeping in the theater through Jeff Chandler, Tony Curtis, Mario Lanza, Mitzi Gaynor, Deborah Kerr, Terry Moore. . . . The hands on the clock would start turning back, and I'd try to imagine what it was like when I was the owner's daughter sleeping in a crib in the balcony of my daddy's palace. How did it feel to be royalty? Once I had a four-hundred-pound usher buying me steaks. Now I had to wait in line for popcorn with everyone else.

Was it possible that Dennis O'Keefe or Spencer Tracy or Michael O'Shea had jumped off the screen and put me in the wrong crib? Sheesh, what a mixup! And no one knows.

I tell you, pal, I'm really a princess.

The Gods Must Be Nasty

I found an inspirational note I wrote to myself some years back. It said: "We learn more from our failures than our successes."

Full of sound and fury, signifying no money. The deal I had lost out on was my 4,444th shot at the big time. A Very Important Guy in a little town called Hollywood had told me to write a short screenplay sample. I'm not sure exactly what the guy did for a living. I think he was some kind of broker/middleman once removed. I know I had read his name in celebrity bios, as in, "Once I found Kenneth, it turned my career around."

Kenneth said I needn't write a long screenplay. "Nobody in L.A. reads," he said, referring to his thirty-nine illiterate friends. "We're all too busy." All I had to do was show him "a sense of beginning-middle-end."

Hey, babe, like, beginning-middle-end is my life.

I'm usually not a procrastinator, but the pressure to make a killing with Kenneth was getting to me. This was when I still believed you had only one shot—instead of a whole barrel of chances—to succeed. And fail.

Then, one moonlit night, I sat down at my word processor and started cooking. It was as if I were on automatic pilot. The bons mots were being delivered like pizza. A scene, a perfect scene—no, make that *the* perfect scene—was being dictated in my ear by an angel from heaven. I was just the vessel. The muse was pouring the sauce.

It was the situation every writer dreams of. I was totally lost in words. It's what we all want from work, from sports, from sex. Is an out-of-body experience really too much to ask for?

After two hours of intense concentration, I woke up to find the word END on my computer screen. Suddenly I realized I was so lost that I had forgotten to press SAVE. When I finally did, a drawing of a bomb appeared on the screen. I was in cosmic doo-doo.

Anyone who has ever seen a Macintosh bomb can tell you that the explosion begins in the pit of your stomach. The greatest story almost ever told—and I lost it.

Now I understood that the muse was not an angel. She was a tease.

I did the only thing possible. I sat there and attempted an instant rewrite of the short screenplay. Although I will never know for sure what glory passed through my screen, the second draft was merely lines recollected in anxiety.

I sent it off to Kenneth, hoping he wouldn't see it for what it was: secondhand prose. Weeks went by, and finally Kenneth called.

"This is great," he said.

"It is?" I said, somewhat taken aback by his buoyant tone. But I listened gleefully as he went on praising the lesser of my two screenplays. All the while I thought: Ha, ha, I got away with it.

"Yes, I think we can interest someone in your work," he said quickly into his car phone. He was on the way to the airport to catch a plane to Paris.

"But what about Spielberg? I thought this was for Spielberg?" I said, having learned to "lose the Steven" in my first conversation with Kenneth.

"Oh, Spielberg only goes with the heavy hitters," he said and hung up somewhere near the X-rated liquor store just outside of LAX.

I rushed up to my husband and recounted the story. "He loved it!" I said. It was only when I got to Kenneth's last line that I realized the whole conversation was a masterful brush-off. An artful rejection. A slap on the hand and a save on the face.

And so my relationship with Kenneth, which had begun like an opening to the heavens and which had sizzled in the middle when I believed I had outsmarted the gods, finally ended with a rude earth landing.

The experience made me feel like a naive little schnook in a big, complicated world. Which is a lesson you can't learn often enough.

Pianotherapy

In my mind I am Alicia Lamour, the recluse chanteuse. I saunter up to the piano and slowly peel my elbow-length white gloves. A rhinestone bracelet dangles from my wrist. My white fox wrap (fake! fake animal fur!) falls to the floor. And in my simple black velvet strapless gown I begin to play "Satin Doll."

Then, switcherooney, I am Patti Page singing "Tennessee Waltz." Segue into Billie Holiday singing "I Cover the Waterfront," then into Barbra Streisand singing the slowest, saddest "Happy Days Are Here Again" that you ever heard. Then I am Linda Ronstadt singing "Blue Bayou," in that opera-singer-with-gallstones voice.

In the real world, the unjust world, I am a woman in a sweatshirt who can't carry a tune. But in the musical world where dreams come true, I am Tina Turner in two feet of skirt and ten feet of legs singing "River Deep, Mountain High."

My kids scream out, "Oh no, Mom, *puh-leeze*, don't sing." My husband forces them to leave the room so the performance can continue. He has learned over time that a badly rendered medley beats an ugly female mood swing any day.

I have always loved to sing and play the piano. Unfortunately, it's my curse to have been given a lousy voice, a tone-deaf ear and no sense of rhythm. But play and sing I must because, hey, Jude, it's the only thing that will make things better.

As a child insomniac, I would wait until everyone was asleep and then at midnight take out my *Hit Parader* magazines and sing "Mockingbird Hill" or "If I Knew You Were Comin' I'd Have Baked a Cake" or "Till I Waltz Again with You" or "The Man in the Raincoat" or "The Wheel of Fortune" until the wee hours of the morning. My bedroom, my pleasant land of counter-pane, became the Club Trocadero where ladies with gardenia corsages and men with thin sterling cigarette cases ate chili con carne and sipped sparkling champagne.

Later, after I took piano lessons, I discovered that when my parents were fighting, music was my only friend. I would sit there banging the ivories until they stopped. I really believed my music had charms.

This was confirmed when I worked as a volunteer at the Berkeley Free Clinic in the sixties. Maybe I couldn't bring down the house with my skills, but I could bring down an acid freakout like nobody's business. I'd just relax and let my fingers do the dancing.

And still today, when I'm sad, if I can just get to that piano, I can save my soul. Sometimes I really am Janis singing "Take a Little Piece of My Heart," and sometimes I'm Frank singing "It Never Entered My Mind," and sometimes I'm Frankie singing "Why Do Fools Fall in Love?" so sweetly that you'd swear the whole world was fourteen years old.

But somehow I am never, ever Little Richard. No matter how hard I try. Imagination has its limits.

Certain songs, like "Wichita Lineman," that I never liked on the radio can sound good to me when performed by Alicia Lamour, while others that I loved, like "I Heard It Through the Grapevine," stink because I'll never be Marvin Gaye. And just because I can't do Jim

Morrison, "Light My Fire" comes out like "In the Good Old Summertime."

The strange thing is that Alicia Lamour can't play and sing in front of other people at all unless they are blood relatives or are OD'ing on drugs. Every once in a while, when I'm really wailing, I'll think: If my friends could see me now. But the few times I've tried to sing for others, it's been a disaster.

When I learned that my mailman, George C. George, had been a musical-comedy star in his youth, I tried to give him a song and dance for Christmas. As he approached my porch, I came out singing and tap-dancing, "It's Mr. George C. George (clap) the mailman . . . bringing me (clap) letters, and maybe (clap) presents, and maybe some (clap) money . . ."

He ran as if he had been attacked by a yelping dog.

But I suppose that has always been the goal of Alicia Lamour, a woman and her music—to make the world go away.

What If They Had a Meeting and Artists Came?

"Hi, my name is Alice, and I'm an artist."

Had I finally found my peer group? That was the question in my mind as I attended my first meeting of Artists Anonymous, a real group in this life that is stranger than satire. The name may sound unnecessary since 99 percent of the world's artists are anonymous. But they couldn't call it Artists, Alas, Anonymous.

The meeting began like other self-help groups, with introductions:

"Hi, my name is Jim, and I'm a musician—this week. . . ."

"My name is Celeste, and I do multimedia. . . ."

"Hi, I'm Mary, and I'm a doll maker. . . ."

It wasn't exactly what I expected. It never exactly is.

What it was was exactly thirty men and women sitting in a circle in a park clubhouse. Average age: I'd guess thirty-seven. Average outfit: gray corduroy slacks, powder-blue turtleneck, maroon zipper jacket. Worn-jogging-shoes-to-sandals ratio, 5:1. One green-haired woman. One black cape.

Although no rule was actually read that forbade us to divulge what went on at the meeting, I assume there is one. But, hey, I can do what I want. I'm an artist. I break all the rules.

Actually, I have no intention of telling specifically

what went on at the meeting. After all, what care you, impatient reader, that Joan began her assemblage that very afternoon? All I can do is tell you why I was there and what my being there means for humanity.

The answers are (1) loneliness and (2) hill of beans, respectively.

What was interesting about this anonymous meeting is that, unlike most groups built around overcoming a compulsion, this one seemed to be designed to help people support their art habit. No one got up and said to wild applause, "Hi, I'm Salvador, and I have been clean and surrealism-free for one year."

Instead, people talked about the torments that stand in the way of the creative process. These include everything from Society to mental blocks to diverting bad habits like drugs and alcohol. Instead of the usual moving story from the speaker about her personal struggle, the speaker at this meeting read from a short story as fine as any I've ever heard.

So what you had was part therapy, part reading, part support group, part dating bar, part networking opportunity, and an incredible place to learn about the latest Matisse show or minimalist music fest.

But had I found my peer group? I am in this strange position of actually getting paid to do creative work. This sounds swell until you consider that it must be done in the confines of a newspaper, meaning it must not be too weird, too dirty, too ethnic, too anything. And they want good, yet.

So, as I listened to people tell tales of trying to get started as artists, the breakthrough-by-fifty-or-bust set, I felt odd. It's my job to lay out my soul for other people to line garbage cans with; yet I felt intimidated talking at a meeting.

I'm cursed and blessed with congenital contrariness.

If I am at a boring party—say, a group of academics—I find it pretty easy to be the life of the party. But here I was in a group of unique, expressive people, and I could hardly say a word.

I was reminded of my childhood fantasy—to be both deeply in the world and yet totally peripheral to it. I wanted to be Tinker Bell. I wanted to be this tiny little invisible fairy who could flit about the universe and see everything, yet go unnoticed.

Hi, my name is Tink, and I'm an artist.

Kind of a Rambo-Hegel
Sort of Thing

Tall and pale and young and handsome, the guy from Yugoslavia came walking. He was my driver, taking me from my sterile corporate Los Angeles hotel to LAX.

"So what do you do when you're not driving a car?" I asked him, knowing that anyone who is young and handsome in L.A. has Big Plans.

"You mean, am I actor?" he said, in a thick Slavic accent. "No, I am not an actor. I am a screenwriter."

"What kind of stuff do you write?" I asked, amused. I had heard that an L.A. newspaper once put a guy out on Melrose Avenue to ask passersby, "How's your screenplay going?" Nine out of ten responded, "Almost finished."

"I write crap. . . ." he said, the way Bela Lugosi says "I am Count Dracula."

I giggled, but he continued in a passionately serious tone.

"I write thrillers. I write the crap that these people want to see," he said, gesturing to the mall/sprawl world we motored through. "What these people want is junk. That's what they line up for. I write that. I do it only for money. That's all I care about is money. When I sell a screenplay, I get two hundred thousand dollars. If I wanted to be Dostoevski, I'd write a book. I want money. That's why I'm here. That's why I write."

He explained that he left Yugoslavia, where he, like his parents, was an intellectual and a writer, to come to the United States. He said no country in the world has as much democracy and freedom as this country.

"And what will you do with all the money?" I asked.

"Ah, that is question, that is very good question," he said. "I don't know."

"So, do you have an agent?" I asked, trying to decide if he was serious.

"No. No agent," he said, "but . . . I know a guy who knows Stallone."

What we had here was a twenty-eight-year-old man with a degree in philosophy from the University of Belgrade who had been in the United States for eighteen months—and already he knew a guy who knew a guy.

"This must be very hard for you, writing in a different culture," I offered. "Are your stories set in Europe?"

"No, I only write about America. It is not hard. I know what to expect when I come here. Nothing surprised me. I drove big American car like this in Yugoslavia. I wrote screenplays there. But they pay nothing —five thousand dollars. Here, you write crap and they give you a lot of money. That's why I come."

"But what about the language problem? Don't you find it hard to write in English?"

"Not a problem," he said, "I write in Serbo-Croatian."

(I was trying to imagine the pitch meeting: "Yo, Stallone, I got piece of crap written in Serbo-Croatian. Perfect for you.")

"So you have a story for Stallone. What's it about?"

"It's about a bodyguard who catches his boss in bed with the president's wife. Then he blackmails him."

If only Nancy Reagan knew Serbo-Croatian, it could be the perfect comeback role.

The handsome screenwriter does, in fact, have a translator. This driver is no idiot, even if he is trying to write crap that stupid Americans would line up to see. He was inspired, he explained, by one of Hegel's greatest hits.

"Have you read Hegel's *Phenomenology of Spirit?*" he asked.

"No," I said. "But I did see *Honey, I Shrunk the Kids.*"

We then talked about the master-servant relationship —as Hegel saw it, as Stallone might develop it.

"But with your attitude," I asked, "don't you think you'll have a problem at a pitch meeting? Isn't ninety-five percent of what goes on in L.A. just sales? You must agree that the best salesmen are those who believe in their product."

"Yes, could be a problem," he admitted, "but I will not tell them it is crap."

This cheered me up. I was well ahead of the game. See, I'm working on a little vehicle for Redford. Kind of a Dan Quayle/Nietzsche thing. It's already in English. And it ain't too bad.

A Writer's Guide to Editorial Fauna

Dear Alice Kahn,

    I write exactly like you. Every thought and feeling you have ever had, I've had too. So how come you're making money at it and I'm not?

        Signed,

        Better-than-you-but-not-published

I'm averaging about one of these letters a week now. I know how you feel. I used to feel that way, too, until I came to understand that publishing is a marketplace, not a meritocracy.

You can't just lay your fish out there. You've got to get the right mackerel to the right frying pan at the right time. You've got to understand the fishmongers, the editors who bring your catch to the public.

As Larry McMurtry says, The difference between life and art is that life has no editor.

It took me a long time to figure out the care and feeding of editors. At first, I saw editors as the people who cut all the good stuff out of my stories, but that was really immature. For instance, I didn't even realize that large organizations like newspapers and magazines have several different species of editors.

Ignoring for a moment the editorial flora, the vegetables who sprout like mushrooms out of oak desk chairs, allow me to present my Field Guide to Editorial Fauna.

First, fighting through the bush, is the Copy Editor —what I like to think of as the Chain Saw Editor. This is the person who does the actual mauling of the story. It is wonderful that our society can find a place for the criminally literal-minded.

There is also the Acquisitions Editor—what I like to call the Manipulations Editor. Unlike the Copy Editor, his hands are clean. (I use the male pronoun only for convenience. There are plenty of vicious, power-hungry women in the editorial jungle.)

The Manipulator, a hunter and gatherer, gets you to do his bidding through a strange combination of flattery, chicanery and the diabolical use of cash. A friend described such editors this way: "They're just like boyfriends in high school. They chase you and chase you, and once you say yes, they have no respect for you."

Finally, there are the Executive Editors—what I like to call the Traveling Editors. These are the people who have gotten where they are through hard work and the ability to give incredible meetings.

They are charming, and you always fall in love with them when they interview you. But like a one-night stand, you never see them again. Instead, they leave a note on your pillow saying: "I've assigned you to Joan, the Manipulations Editor, who will get Wilbur, the Chain Saw Editor, to go over your work. Wilbur comes to us from the Shredding Room of the National Security Council. If you need me, I'll be in Denver next week."

There are a few tricks for taming the editor. Here are my suggestions to keep the beast at bay:

1. All editors want is a sensational, controversial story that shocks everyone while offending no one.

2. Remember when Lou Grant told Mary Richards, "You know what you've got? You've got spunk . . . I

hate spunk." Most editors actually love spunk—especially in a woman. What they don't like is a woman with balls.

3. Editors always love a joke about their hometown. If you find out your editor is from Des Moines and you slip a Des Moines joke in a story, he'll think you're Shakespeare.

4a. Editors are supersmart, the only people smart enough to understand how stupid and shallow the readers are. That's why they will always tell you: "I love this story, but the readers won't understand it, so we're axing it."

4b. Editors are also the Nielsen Family of cultural literacy. When they don't get something, they will tell you that the average Joe won't get it either. But a writer must never question the schizophrenia of the editor by wondering how someone can be both the pinnacle of knowledge and the lowest common denominator.

What can I tell you about the editor-patient relationship? Here are some of the ways editors manipulate writers:

1. Editors use sibling rivalry every chance they get, telling one writer how great another writer is. This drives us nuts.

2. Editors constantly remind us about the huge pile of free-lance submissions waiting on their desks. They don't actually come out and say the sea is crawling with sharks and they all have home computers.

3. Editors keep telling us how terrific a piece that we did three years ago was. The idea is, if you can only uncover another Major Trend or discover the next Faith Popcorn, you might still have a career.

4. Editors like to flash the poor circulation figures of competitors, as if to say: "If you don't like the editing

here, you can leave . . . but nobody will ever read you again."

5. After a successful story, when the writer is feeling full of herself, the editor likes to point out a few humiliating spelling errors. My editor practices the Socratic method of editing:

HE: Did you mean to spell Nathanael West that way?

ME: I know West spelled Nathanael some weird way.

HE: Did he spell it *that* weird way?

6. Editors like to print grotesque attacks on the writer in the letters column. But they will dismiss the fan mail, saying they don't want to print it and appear self-promoting. (Once a paper printed a letter about my column under the headline "A Disgrace.")

But I'd hate to leave you with the impression that I'm down on editors. I have a very good relationship with mine. The section of the paper I write for has one contributor who is a convict in a federal penitentiary. I like to show my editor that I know my place by referring to myself as "your other prisoner."

Money Can't
Buy You Acreage

We were heading toward Rancho Mucho Dinero, my friend Peter and I. We were doing what people do for kicks these days. See, we don't do drugs. We don't do cholesterol. We do open houses.

Rancho Mucho is the name I have given to a certain development of million-dollar-plus houses an hour out of town where civilization and water once stopped. There, in that arid, godforsaken place, we suddenly came to a faux lake, a faux creek and a faux waterfall. We are about to enter an entire faux universe.

To get through the locked gates, we must first visit the sales office. "Wait a minute," says Peter. "What's our story?"

"No story," I tell him. "I'll just say my husband, Shlomo, and I are looking for a nice Hasidic community. . . ."

In the sales office, standing beneath a huge poster showing the security patrol that protects Rancho Mucho, is a latter-day suburban salesman. His impeccable dress is marred only by his dragon breath. He tells us that there are no open houses today but we can drive around and look at the full range of properties in the Rancho Mucho community. It turns out the place is well stocked with less publicized cheapos.

We could start with the $300,000 townhomes in the

Point Negras Blancas area. "They'll be selling for four hundred thousand in six months," the salesman warns. If they're still standing.

I began to wonder if the million-dollar jobs were the loss leaders for these mass items.

Next, we could visit the Vista Del Visa pool homes, right there on the main road and priced to move at $750,000. And, finally, old fire-breath suggests, we could drive up toward the million-dollar customized homes on "the Gold Coast."

Coast? What Coast? The nearest body of water is eighty miles west.

We cruise the dry coast but can only press our noses at a locked gate within the gates. Here, a gardener points out the manor house up on the hill, a thirty-thousand-square-foot hacienda that the developer of Rancho Mucho has built for himself. "The bedroom is forty-eight hundred square feet," says the gardener. Then he adds, laughing, "I don't know what they do there."

He is busy working on the faux green lawn of a big pink Mediterranean, where a brass plaque announces that the house is entitled: "Una Espressione d'Amore."

We stop off at Rancho Mucho's own supermarket, Alpha Mucho, which has items ranging from a little bag of potato chips to a nine-liter bottle of Moët & Chandon for 475 big ones. In the corner of the black-and-white tiled floor, a pianist plays a grand piano that is parked near the veggies. I recognize the Muzakified strains of an old Beatles tune: "Can't Buy Me Love."

A few days later, I come back to the open houses. I must see what lurks behind the faux-Tudor exteriors. This time I bring my real husband instead of my faux husband.

During the time between my first and my second visit to this real estate Disneyland, I have reread *The Great*

Gatsby, Fitzgerald's saga about a guy with a mansion trying to win the love of a gal. Gatsby's pad is an "imitation of some Hotel de Ville in Normandy, with a tower on one side . . . and a marble swimming pool and more than forty acres of lawn and garden."

The houses at Rancho Mucho are no less pretentious but sit on small lots, one on top of the other, your Jacuzzi up against your neighbor's wet bar.

In the wine cellar of an executive Georgian, I inspect a case of bottles stacked on its side. The label reads, "Cheap Red Wine."

My husband notes the high-voltage line running directly over a 1985 antebellum mansion. He looks up from the veranda and says, "Five bedrooms, a pool, a fur closet and cancer."

Every house has a library—a man's room, all in dark wood with bar, mahogany desk, leather desk set and wooden duck decoys. I had heard that the books weren't real or that they were painted-on faux libraries. Or perhaps the volumes were acquired from some "Books by the Yard" discount store. But the books I saw were real. Each house had a well-worn copy of *Iacocca* among the untouched leather sets.

I thought about a scene in *The Great Gatsby* set in Gatsby's "high Gothic library, panelled with carved English oak, and probably transported complete from some ruin overseas." There, a drunken man is raving about the books. He says, "Absolutely real—have pages and everything. I thought they'd be of a nice durable cardboard. . . . He didn't cut the pages but what do you want? What do you expect?"

After looking at three of these houses, my husband began to get ill. He compared it to mall syndrome and thought the decaying formaldehyde in the building materials was getting to him. "I hate the twentieth century," he said as we drove off the faux bridge at Rancho Mucho.

But I think what was really sickening him was the thought that this was all a million dollars gets you these days. That's why the middle class loves to laugh at the nouveau riche. All that effort for so little more. You can't be a Great Gatsby; you can only be a tract Gatsby.

It's a faux world after all.

The Pauline Kael of Porn

Remember what it was like to be a little girl and have a "dirty book"? I'll never forget the day my mother found mine. "This is for morons!" she said, and took away my illustrated copy of Voltaire's *Candide*.

I guess that's why I was pleasantly surprised by Susie Bright. She certainly didn't fit my mother's definition of a "moron." With her harlequin glasses, floral print dress, red high heels and hair pulled back in a bun, Bright looked like a stylish librarian.

She told me she is a lesbian, a feminist and a nerd. Big deal—this is San Francisco. What is unique is her job. Susie Bright is the porno movie reviewer for *Forum* magazine.

For the past year, her witty and literate column, "The Erotic Screen: The Cream of Adult Videos," has proven her the Pauline Kael of porn. Says Susie, "I think we need to develop a professional attitude toward pornography in order to understand it and, in fact, to demand more from it."

Her $700-per-column job supports her real love, publication of a magazine called *On Our Backs*. I gave away my prejudices when I entered the *On Our Backs* office on Castro Street. Noting the immaculate office, the white furniture and *The New York Times Book Review*, I blurted out, "My God, this is clean!"

"You expected a dirty magazine to have a dirty office?" asked Susie.

I said nothing about the receptionist's lunch sitting on the front desk—a large banana wrapped in plastic.

Susie Bright sees herself as part of the "new wave of erotic literacy" brought on by the increasing involvement of women in the pornography industry. "Distribution is the key to who controls porn," she said. "Most of the current distributors are conservative themselves, not very sexually knowledgeable."

Criminalizing porn, she continued, also harms the industry, as does the anti-porn faction in the women's movement, what Bright calls "the fundamentalist feminists."

Bright thinks porn liberation has gotten a boost from an unexpected source. "People who try to repress pornography contribute to opening it up," she says. "Thanks to Ed Meese, we can now say 'bondage' on TV."

According to Bright, many people in the pornography industry come from fundamentalist backgrounds. But not Bright herself. Born in 1958, she grew up in a liberal family, eager to take her place in the social revolution of the sixties. "The whole thing slipped away while I was in high school."

By the time she got to college, the only really exciting thing on campus, she says, was gay liberation. She went to UC Santa Cruz, "home of the creative major," and got a degree in Community Organizing Around Sexual Politics. (It could have been worse. She could have majored in physics around quantum mechanics.)

"I wanted to be politically correct in my sexual liberation," she said. "I wanted to have feminist sex. That made me shy. Feminism knows about sexism. They don't know shit about sex.

"Feminism also contributed to men feeling guilty about sex," she adds. "Men who were pornophiles but not monsters weren't prepared to deal with the criticism."

Susie says she was so into politically correct sex that for a while she had sex only with "members of the same Communist sect." Her doctrinaire background occasionally slips into her prose, like when she talks about porno actors grabbing "the means of production."

Today, even her father, a linguistics professor at UCLA, supports her work and subscribes to her magazine. But her mother, according to Bright, "feels it is a tragedy."

In her reviews, Bright tries to find what is valuable in commercial porn. "There's nothing easier than to put it down, but I try to home in on what is there for me. To see if my body says something my mind doesn't." She notes that most porno reviewers sound like ad copy. "They say things like: 'It's hot! It's wild! Bimbo of the Year! Mr. Shlong! . . .'"

I ask her if she sees any contradiction in reviewing porn for a straight audience.

"People understand that what turns you on in food and clothes doesn't turn everyone else on. But with sex, people are illiberal, people are ignorant. In fact, people are dying now because of sexual ignorance."

Bright recently made her screen debut as an extra in *Behind the Green Door II*, a movie she says is "not as hot as some but is unusual in what it highlights—it shows you can get turned on by safe sex."

Most porno movies, according to Bright, deal with common fantasies—the more taboo the better.

She says recent research by Masters and Johnson shows that the second most common fantasy is "forceful taking or being forcefully taken." But she disagrees with those who say that movies showing rape fantasies cause violence to women. "They only inspire a psychotic. Most of us are brought up to understand what is real and what is pretend. Men, too, have these fantasies of being taken. You hear it all the time on 'The Dating Game' and 'Love Connection.' "

She says the most common fantasy is sex with someone other than your normal partner, and this forms the basis for most pornography. "Porn will take you by surprise by serving up the clichés in some new way. There's a whole genre about sex between enormously fat women and skinny men made by Big Top Videos. I was amazed by how one of these affected me."

Bright says her favorite porno film is called *Smoker*, made by Veronica Rocket, a man-and-woman team. "It held my attention from beginning to end, unlike most porn, where you have to fast-forward to the good scene." The key scene in this movie showed a cross-dresser trying on his former girlfriend's blue silk slip. "I cried when I watched it," says Bright. "It was so nostalgic. It was art. Ideally, a porn movie should touch me artistically and get me off."

Watching porn has made her more astute about watching conventional movies. "Conventional movies are masters of foreplay," she says. In this regard, she thought *Witness*, a suspense story involving an Amish family, was one of the sexiest movies she'd ever seen.

What Bright hates in conventional movies is violence. "I can't even watch a Visine commercial—you know, when the woman sticks the stuff in her eye." I found this squeamishness hard to square with the pictures in Susie's magazine—pictures of piercing jewelry that made me cringe.

Perhaps her most telling comment was when I asked

her what she found decadent. "You mean like, 'Let's go jump into a vat of chocolate'?"

Although she did not make a pornophile out of me, I can appreciate someone like Susie Bright, someone with a mind so open you can sail the Mediterranean fleet through it.

Coming of Age
with the Niners

The battle I saw is now ancient history. Yet the civilization I speak of rises again each Sunday morning.

I arrived at the desolate precipice known to pilgrims as "the Stick" with only my faithful guide, Macho Kinti, and a primitive knowledge of the culture of football.

I had attended an urban Jewish high school where our varsity squad, the Woody Allens (also known as the Bulldogs), was regularly hounded by the Dobermans of this world. They never won during the entire four years I witnessed their pathetic performances. At the University of Illinois, during the season I attended every game, the fighting Illini scored only one TD.

I became convinced that it was *my* presence that hurt whatever team I cared about. I vowed never to lay my evil eye on football again.

I worried about the 49ers when I started to watch them on television. Since they seemed to be doing so well despite my support, I thought the jinx was broken and I could attend a professional football game.

Macho Kinti and I approached the parking lot. A red sea of 49er shirts and great big bellies parted to admit us. We were in the Niner soup now.

The faithful were gathered in little tribes among the Winnebagos, Chieftains, Open Roaders and Sportscoaches. They sat at picnic tables with red-checkered cloths around sizzling barbecue fires rubbing bottles with genies named St. Pauli Girl, Gibley's and Corona. On a typical table, little boxes were lined up as offerings: Triscuits, Wheat Thins, Veggie Thins, Crispy Lights and Ritz.

There was a van with framed paintings of John Wayne parked near a classic Caddie with a 49ers grille ornament next to a Mercedes sedan. In this culture, the car is the temple of the soul.

Mike Pasco had arrived at eight-thirty that morning, four and a half hours before game time. He wanted to get a choice spot for his fire-engine red Dodge Power Wagon, which was mounted on enormous tires called Gumbo Monster Mudders.

Not to be outdone was Tim McCoy, whose "Gold Rush Red" truck had been featured in *Pickups and Mini-Trucks*, *Van Digest* and *4WD* magazine. He had a blowup of the magazine photo of his truck—"personally autographed by the Forty-niners." It was on display next to a lawn chair, which was crocheted with 49er insignia. McCoy has been to every home game for sixteen years.

Inside the stadium, I left Macho Kinti with our repast of baguette, fromage and mineral water. We seemed to be stuck in the yuppie-niner section—far from the marijuana-smoking, beer-guzzling, butt-kicking masses. I went out to find some real Americans.

I talked to Mike Busselman, a golf-course grounds-keeper. He came alone by bus and considers coming to these games his "biggest priority." The highlight of his 49er fan career was during the '81 Dallas play-offs "when a guy stood on top of the fence and went berserk."

Busselman is wearing a 49ers hat covered with 49ers pins. He is wearing a 49ers shirt and a 49ers jacket. I leave him at the souvenir stand where he is purchasing a 49ers pen.

Tammie Bishop, a property manager, is there with her boyfriend. She had a conversion experience while watching the '81 Dallas game at Clint Eastwood's Hog's Breath Inn in Carmel. She's been coming ever since. Her favorite moment in a game is "after they sing the national anthem and everybody yells."

Michael Wild, owner of the Bay Wolf Cafe and an accomplished chef, was there, looking for something to eat. He recommended the hot dog. "Food tastes good in context," he said, "and this hot dog, which would taste lousy anyplace else, tastes great here." And I thought I was the only anthropologist in the arena.

The true test of scientific detachment would come in the stands. Could I just sit there like a data-gathering lump when the joint started jumping?

Why come to the game if not to participate in the roar? To chant "Dee-fense, Dee-fense, Dee-fense," to form the high-energy ahm-m-m-m that causes the stadium to vibrate, to roll with the great mandala of football, to see a guy go berserk, to go berserk—that's why they're here, that's why I'm here. People sitting in the stands watching the game on little televisions haven't paid twenty-one dollars to see the game. They have paid to be a part of the psychodrama.

The cheerleaders take their places on the field. Once apple-cheeked home-girl rooters, they are now Vegas show girls performing T & A shimmies for the largely male crowd. This is no place to be Margaret Mead.

"When did cheerleaders start cultivating the slut look?" I ask Macho Kinti. "Come on," he says, "they're hardly the Raiderettes."

And the players are hardly the gladiators of the TV screen. Jeff Kemp (filling in for ailing superstar Joe Montana) is a shrimp. Kinti points out Moroski, Kemp's understudy, and tells me he is a Marin County boy. Players from Marin County and Dartmouth—"Isn't that un-usual?" I ask my guide. "No," the trusty Kinti answers, "quarterbacks can be sissies."

Lined up around the ball, the players look like little robots. Their tiny heads are lost in helmets, their shoulders padded like Transformer toys, their vulnerable joints surrounded by armor. Only the soft round prominence of their buttocks reminds us of their humanity.

But the stands are bulging with humanity, barely contained in their seats. I remarked to Kinti—who told me to shut up—that the cultural experience was halfway between McDonald's and a Grateful Dead concert. Like McDonald's, almost everything in the environment is clean, orderly and reasonably predictable. Like a Dead show, at any minute the guy next to you might stand up and freak out. But should the freakout get too heavy, red-coated ushers, yellow-jacketed Event Staff, royal-blue security and dark blue SFPD are everywhere. A rainbow of reassurance.

I watched Kimo Laihipp look up from his TV and start leading cheers. He wore a big red Stetson with a 49ers doll and buttons on it that said, "Dallas, Eat Shit and Die," "Colts, Eat Shit and Die," and the ever popular "Bullshit." For each unfavorable call, Laihipp would point to this button and lead the crowd in chants of derision. In his other life, Laihipp runs a Silicon Valley consulting firm and is downright normal.

Under the influence of beer and Laihipp, my scientific objectivity wavers. Will I be shaken to my pretentious roots, drawn into the cult of yahoo, because it is, after all—fun?

When the team scores, when Kemp sails the ball to Rice, it is heaven. Men stand erect, their arms tautly supporting clenched fists. Women kiss their partners. Macho Kinti smiles at me. Kemp embraces Rice. There is joyous butt slapping among the players on the side-lines.

Only coach Bill Walsh continues to look deadly serious, cross-armed, pacing—the good white Volvo-ed expectant father.

Soon my notes begin to stray. "Intoxicated Tuiasosopo leaps into the air, recalling Nureyev mid-tour jeté." Later: "Silence/shadow of a hawk over field/Craig receives/Joy." Are the other fans writing ersatz haiku in their notebooks?

The game seems to be in the bag. The mood has turned upbeat. Smiles flash, beer bottles flow, shirts come off. Then I ruin it all.

I turn to Macho Kinti and say, "I hope the Vikings score so the game is more exciting."

Fourth quarter, two-minute warning, the game is tied. "Vikings suck," a fan yells.

"You wanted excitement," Kinti says with disgust. Once again the anthropologist has modified the tribal rituals.

We race to the bathrooms. I am almost tackled by a huge man racing to his beer-induced rendezvous with destiny. From another subculture, Kinti reports that in the men's room the guy next to him at the crowded trough asked, "What is this, a drug test?"

As the game goes into overtime, I put down my note-book. "Stop him," we scream. "Kill him."

"Football sucks," screams an old boy in a Niners cap and jacket.

After the fall, fans file out silently. "They should've won," says a man as his girlfriend rubs his back consolingly. Some still remain in their seats in a daze.

"It's your fault," Macho Kinti tells me.

We walk through the parking lot, among the little mounds of burnt charcoal, reminders of the civilization that once flourished here. Judging from the scraps of paper on the shards of broken glass, its name was: Budweiser.

As we drive out past the True Hope Church of Christ and the Rock of Ages Baptist Church in one of San Francisco's poorest neighborhoods, I tell my guide, "Losing is an interesting emotion."

"We get to lose all week," he says. "The weekends are supposed to be for winning."

Columnist Is a Tramp

In which I attempt to respond to the following real letter that came in the real mail.

Editorial Dept.
San Francisco Chronicle
San Francisco, CA

Dear Editors,

As a former professional cheerleader with the San Francisco 49ers, I found Alice Kahn's reference to this year's 49er cheerleading squad in her article "Coming of Age with the Niners" to be extremely offensive and demeaning.

Kahn asked the question, "When did cheerleaders start cultivating the slut look?" The answer, Ms. Kahn, is never. Neither the current 49er squads nor those in the past have ever conveyed this look or reflected this attitude.

The 49er cheerleading teams, under the direction of the United Spirit Association, are dedicated to provide a class-act form of entertainment. Each team member adheres to a strict ethical code of conduct and the routines which Kahn referred to as "T and A" moves are anything but this. All choreography is carefully planned to reflect a polished series of dance moves and the uniforms, which project an athletic image, are among the most conservative outfits in the N.F.L.

As far as appealing solely to a male audience, I'd like you to note, Ms. Kahn, that I've received an equal amount of compliments from both men and women who are thankful for this dedication to quality which the 49er squads possess.

Personally, what I find most offensive is the stereo-typical implication that cheerleaders are slut-like. I, along with all of my teammates, have worked hard over the years to erase this limited mentality that all cheer-leaders are loose and air-headed.

Nearly every girl on our past teams was an honors student in high school or college and the term loose could not be tagged on *any* one of us.

No, Ms. Kahn, the only thing I find "slut"-like about the entire matter is the prostitution of journalism ethics you evidenced when you failed to get the facts and in-stead resorted to subjective slander.

Sincerely,

Dear Sincerely,

I sincerely apologize for implying the 49er cheerlead-ers looked slut-like. Of course, objectively speaking, they are just scantily clad women with large breasts. . . .

Dear Sincerely,

I'm afraid we have had a misunderstanding. Or should I say a *Ms.* understanding? (Just kidding!) The emphasis in my comment is on the word "look." A slut *look* no more implies that a woman is a slut than a "class-act form of entertainment" implies an act has class. . . .

Dear Sincerely,

I couldn't agree with you more when you say the 49er cheerleader outfits "are among the most conservative outfits in the N.F.L." Did not my guide to football, Macho Kinti, observe in the same story from which you quote that "they're hardly the Raiderettes." By the way, where in the heck do you think those Raiderettes get their outfits? Frederick's of the Tenderloin? . . .

Dear Sincerely,
    I owe you an apology. In referring to the 49er cheer-leaders act as T & A, I in no way meant to suggest that your choreographer, Louie Baryshnikov, hadn't care-fully planned a polished series of T & A moves. . . .

Dear Sincerely,
    I'm glad women appreciate the dedication to quality of the 49er squad as well as men do. With so many men ready to see us women as some kind of dancing meat, I suppose I've come across to you as a traitor, an Aunt Tom, a wolf in Saks clothing. But I never said women didn't like the 49er cheerleaders. They just weren't spil-ling beer on their pants and leering like the male fans. . . .

Dear Sincerely,
    Nobody actually called anybody "loose." I would never tag the term "loose" on anybody. "Like a bunny" is more in keeping with my prose style. . . .

Dear Since,
    Loosen up, baby. . . .

Listen, Sincerely,
    As a former honor student myself, I found your ste-reotype offensive. Being good at school in no way implies that a gal won't put out. . . .

Ms. Sincerely,

As a feminist, I take exception to your use of the word "girl" to describe these honor students who are working their T's and A's off. Who better deserves the designation "woman"? . . .

Look, Lady,

How dare you say that I have prostituted my journalism ethics? I have no journalism ethics. . . .

Sincerely Dearest,

Making fun is a dirty business. But some slut's got to do it.

Yours for union wages,

Alice Kahn

Life Is Short, but
Art Can Take All Night

It seemed a simple enough request. A magazine had called and asked me to do a story. After I wrote the story, they asked if I would pose for a photograph to illustrate it. I said yes. Foolish me. Little did I suspect that I had unwittingly plunged myself into the Valley of Art Psychosis.

I understand that photography is an Art, that it takes time, that it requires a genius who can walk that tightrope between technology and ecstasy.

The photographer called every night for a week telling me to hold on—he was scouting for the *right* setting. When he said he wouldn't do the shoot until he found just the right setting, I began to smell an Art rat.

I don't enjoy looking at photographs of myself. My father refused to have his photograph taken because he, like the Indians, believed that the camera captured your spirit. I don't like having my picture taken because I believe the camera captures your image.

See, I have this little problem. I'm not Christie Brinkley. Not that I want to be Christie Brinkley or think like Christie Brinkley or even write like Christie Brinkley. I don't want to be married to Billy Joel. I just honestly wouldn't mind looking like Christie Brinkley for the purposes of having my photograph taken.

If you think I've been brainwashed into some media

idea of young blond beauty, let me put it a different way. I wouldn't mind looking like Tina Turner either.

But OK. In a careless moment, I agreed to set aside my vanity and allow my image and spirit to be captured. I did *not* agree to become an Art victim.

I suspected that had happened when the photographer called to say I was to meet him on a high and windy hill at dusk and then on a low and languid beach at five o'clock the next morning.

I gave him dusk but not dawn. He responded as if I were trying to sabotage his Art. I came back with the fact that he was trying to sabotage my life as a Working Mother.

Did I mention that he also complained about how little he was getting paid for his Art and that he had to split that with his agent?

So I stood on the high and windy hill at dusk and posed as he called out commandments to me and his three assistants. "Look natural or it won't work," he shouted as he checked his lights and power generator and blockaded a quiet residential street. "Smile right at me," he called as passersby gathered to watch us. One passerby asked me in disbelief, "Are you a professional model?"

I acquiesced when he asked me to change my shirt and move to yet another location and stand with my legs crossed on a sloping hill, placing my weight on a large umbrella he handed me. And smile. As I did this, one assistant was to throw an orange motorcycle helmet across the photograph to another assistant.

Why?

That was the Art part.

The photographer kept yelling at the assistants, who were throwing the helmet too high or too low. It had to be *just* right. After several shots, the Nikon Leonardo suddenly threw up his hands and said, "That's it. The light's gone. We don't have a picture."

"You do have a picture," I screamed at him. He had two hundred pictures. None of them were just right. None of them were Art. But we were talking magazine here, not Sistine Chapel.

"Look, man, it's a gig," I said, attempting to speak the parlance of artists. "You did it. I don't want to go through this again."

He looked at me as if I were the queen of the Philistines, a barrier between him and the creative process.

Now, if this guy wants to create Art all by himself and drive himself nuts and cut off his ear, that's fine with me. Indeed, I occasionally attempt Art myself, but that is a private act between a consenting adult and her word processor.

Picasso had wives to kick around. Andrew Wyeth had Helga. Sonny had Cher. But this poor guy didn't have me.

And that is why you won't see "Journalist with Motorcycle Helmet" hanging in the Louvre anytime soon.

two

The TEMPLE

of LIFESTYLE

"Biff,"
a Celebrity Drug Abuser

It was a brilliant California morning as I approached the Rodeo Drive offices of "Biff an Ex–Crack User Inc." The waiting room was already filling with others hoping for a crack at Biff himself.

The receptionist, one of those gorgeous ex–homecoming queens from Iowa, was busy answering the phone. Her exquisitely manicured nails clicked down on the various buttons as she said, "Biff-an-Ex-Crack-User . . . can you hold?"

Taking advantage of a lull in the phone storm, I approached the bench.

"Excuse, me," I said, "I'm Kahn from the *Chronicle*. I have a nine-thirty appointment with Biff."

"Look, we've got Bob Greene in there now," she said. "A film crew from ABC is setting up, and we got *People* magazine coming in after that. You're going to have to wait your turn. Here's your packet."

A painted talon immediately hit a button. "I'm sorry, Mr. Rather. Biff can't make the follow-up for 'Crackdown on Crack Street.' He'll be in Boston signing copies of *Don't Knock the Rock Until It Knocks You: The True Story of Biff an Ex–Crack User*. Maybe another time."

I sank into the plush white chair and looked at the packet. On the cover of the mauve folder was a silver-embossed silhouette of a man and the words: "Biff an

Ex–Crack User." Inside were various sheets of paper on the stationery of Gurwitz and Hurwitt, Communications Consultants, and several glossy photographs of Biff.

Some of the photos in the packet were shot from behind. One, with a child, was shot in darkened silhouette; another showed a fit, attractive man in skimpy bathing trunks with a black rectangle over his face. The back of each photo was stamped: "For availability contact Biff an Ex–Crack User (213) 447-CRAK."

I looked at the sheet of paper headed "Quotations from Biff an Ex–Crack User. EDUCATED, ARTICULATE, AUTHENTIC." Each quotation was preceded by a silver bullet:

• "I was ready to lay down my life for a PIECE of the rock."

• "CRACK will destroy your life like it destroyed mine."

• "Once I had a wife, kids, a successful job, a beautiful 4-bedroom, 3½-bath home with attached garage, a timeshare at Tahoe and a turbo Porsche. Now all I've got are memories and a CONDO in Westwood."

I continued reading the packet, but I was getting IMPATIENT. It was past ten-thirty. Greene had walked out. The ABC crew had come and gone. Still no Biff. I approached the ex-Iowa-homecoming-queen-turned-would-be-Hollywood-starlet, but got nowhere.

"You'll just have to wait. Biff is a very busy man," she said, and the talon descended to the third button. "Bill Graham Presents? I think Biff can make 'Rock Against the Rock' in San Francisco next month, but it'll cost you an extra ten bills if you want him to sing."

Although I was close to Biff burnout, I went back to

my packet and picked up the sheet labeled: "Curriculum Vitae of Biff an Ex–Crack User."

1965–69 BA cum laude, Yale University
    Thesis: "New Criticism of Olde English"
    1968 Whiffenpoofs' World Tour
1969–71 MBA Wharton School of Business
    Began smoking MARIJUANA every day
1971 Management Trainee of a MAJOR Business Machines Corporation
    Occasional LSD use
1972–76 Product Development of another MAJOR Company
    Occasional use of QUAALUDES
1976–79 Princeton Institute for Advanced Study
    First SNORTED cocaine
1980 Married to "Bets," Holyoke '72
1981 Boston Marathon
1982 Twins Bud and Bub born
    Regular COKE and LUDES use
1982 Vice President Own Computer Products Firm, Cupertino, CA.
    Son Dusty born
    FREEBASING
1985 $600-a-Day CRACK Habit

I looked up as the door to the inner office flew open. An attractive man in his late thirties wearing a blue blazer, white slacks and a black Lone Ranger mask dashed out. I stomped up to the receptionist.

"Was that Biff?" I asked, ready to give her hell.

"I'm afraid it was. We had an emergency," she said without batting a fake eyelash.

"What the hell kind of emergency does a celebrity drug addict have?" I demanded to know.

"Mrs. Reagan called to say she was in the neighborhood shopping and she had to meet Biff."

"But I had an appointment," I said.

"I'm sorry," she said with a flip of the wrist, "but when Nancy Reagan calls, you can't just say no."

Born-Again Hetero

Nora Freeman (not her real name) is using her old name again. She's also tinting her hair, wearing press-on nails and exaggerating her lipline with sensual Revlon red.

She's got an old man and is also seeing a younger man. At forty, she's considering her first pregnancy. In her padded-shoulder jacket, her long, straight slit skirt and pointy toe pumps, she looks like Today's New Pulled-Together Woman.

I knew her when she was Thunder Freewoman (also not her real name). She was then a militant radical feminist lesbian, a self-described "stone dyke." She offers no explanation for her conversion back to heterosexuality other than, "The times change, people change."

And I used to laugh when people described themselves as "cultural lesbians."

We reminisced about the old days over smoked chicken salad in the Cafe California. I kept flashing back to Thunder as she was then, with her waist-length hair flowing, and her well-trained biceps bulging from beneath her tank top, and her impressive anger, which she was always in touch with. Today, the anger seems gone except when she pushes a pile of bangs off her forehead and complains that her "mousse went flat by ten o'clock."

I remember the endless bull sessions—or did we call them cow sessions?—when each of us would discuss her *her*story. Some told terrible stories about abusive or self-ish fathers and husbands. Others described how they oppressed themselves with hair rollers and diets and shoes reminiscent of foot-binding.

Thunder shocked the group by pulling out a photo of herself as she appeared "before liberation"—a bronze, bikini-clad surfer girl on the sands of Santa Monica.

We were the Women's Health Collective, a group I explained in our 1972 literature with the following sen-tence: "We are an organization of 90 politically radical women dedicated to smashing macho and inhumanity by organizing around the issue of health." Around the issue indeed.

At the time, I privately described the group this way: Some came for the women, some came for the health and some came for the collective. That is, some joined just to be part of a group, some joined because they had health problems or were interested in health careers, and some came because they were interested in lesbianism.

Those of us in the group who were straight were un-comfortable with third-sex issues because we felt it ste-reotyped feminists.

Of course, at that time styles traditionally considered "masculine" were all the rage—pants, no makeup, flat shoes, the short curly haircut known as the "lib frizz." We insisted that feminists could still be "feminine" with-out the traditional outward signs.

On the other hand, none of us wanted to be labeled "straight," which in the mood of those times was uncool, a little like being a racist.

Thunder insisted that we make a statement support-ing "the lesbian nation." She raised the issue at a special all-day all-collective meeting to decide What We Believe.

We were drafting one of our interminable position papers on "our collective politics and priorities."

It was a meeting I won't soon forget. Not because of the radical issues or outrageous topics that were discussed but because half the women were nude.

Filmmaker Lawrence Kasdan once said he had shot a scene for the movie *The Big Chill* showing the characters as they were fifteen years earlier. He said that he decided not to use it because no one who hadn't been there would believe what had gone on. When I read Kasdan's remarks in an interview, I immediately flashed back to the clothes-optional political discussion.

It was a sign of how behaviorally loose the times were that no one recognized she was actually making a statement by stripping.

It all seemed so natural: The meeting was held outdoors in a backyard, and when the fog burned off, those who wore their corduroy bells and black turtlenecks were roasting. As the stripping began, everyone was cool. No one batted an eyelash. One by one, the participants went topless and then bottomless—all the while discussing "how to demystify medical practices which alienate us from our bodies and maintain the hierarchical distribution of medical knowledge."

I do remember that Thunder was there, saying important things about demystification, although I have no recollection of what she actually said.

My friend Fran summed up our soul-searching: "Everyone was so serious, but what I kept noticing was who still shaved her legs." Thunder was one of those closet straights.

I thought of this as Nora-née-Thunder's limp wrist, covered with silver bracelets, dangled over her chicken salad. She was trying to scrape off the mayo so there would be fewer calories. As I looked around the room, I realized you couldn't tell a feminist from a hooker anymore. Only their hairdressers know for sure.

"I'm thinking of getting my body waxed," she said.

When Thunder goes straight, she does it with a vengeance.

As goes feminism, so goes the lesbian nation. Someone I once knew as a militant lesbian now shrugs her shoulders and says, "I was always basically straight." Was it the zeal of the convert or just another college fad?

Maybe I am Ms. Priss, but I'm a little awed by the cultural promiscuity of my generation. Just when you get used to everybody coming out, they start going back in.

A Man's Home
Is His Restaurant

Like leaves in the wind, we drifted into The Cellar at Macy's. And they call the wind Jeremiah.

We were there to see celebrity chef Jeremiah Tower turn fish into gold.

Jeremiah towered above an audience of thirty-five seated admirers. At least three times that many were standing in the aisles among the Krups Mini Espresso Makers and the cappuccino machines.

(In 1983, when I wrote a piece of satire called "Yuppies," I described a couple who woke up and turned on the Signor Cappuccino. I thought it was a joke. But just as life imitates art, Macy's imitates satire.)

Jeremiah, who in any decent society would be a tenured professor of art history, was slaving over a slab of salmon. Like a voyeur in a Vegas motel room, I could watch everything he did to it reflected in a huge overhead mirror.

At his side was his assistant, Michael Eggert, a chef-in-training. Like his boss, he was impeccably attired in chef's clothing. Eggert is also a law student. In case the chef thing doesn't work out, he can always switch to wolf's clothing.

While Jeremiah stuck salt, peppercorns and fresh dill into the salmon, thereby turning it into gravlax, Michael played the magician's assistant. "This is why I have a restaurant," said Jeremiah. "There's always someone around to clean up." The man can prepare a platter and keep up a patter. No Jerry Ford, he.

A frequent theme of Jeremiah Tower's chatter was the need for first-class stuff. "It's hard to buy decent-quality smoked salmon retail. If you can spend the money, get the best salmon you can." . . . "Buy expensive plastic wrap, the cheap ones smell." . . . "Look at this halibut, see how it glows." . . . "You can't have an urban life or The Met Life without fresh herbs."

The Met Life was what the demonstration was all about. It is a national promotional venture between *Metropolitan Home* magazine and department stores like Macy's that sell the products needed for The Met Life. In addition to samples of Jeremiah Tower's cooking, the audience also got free copies of the magazine.

Metropolitan Home is the bible of what demographer Faith Popcorn calls "cocooning," the trend of baby boomers staying home. Part of this trend is not just making the home a castle but turning every bit of the home life into a work of art. Cooking ranks high, and celebrity chefs such as Tower, L.A.'s Wolfgang Puck and Berkeley's Alice Waters are frequently quoted as gurus of the domestic-arts movement.

The editor of *Metropolitan Home* says her concept is "about people like you, captured in the midst of *becoming* rather than being, in the midst of sorting out what really matters. Living The Met Life is about making choices. It's even about all those embarrassing '80s terms that make us wince: lifestyle (ouch), mind-set, options, commitment, caring, and what happened to the Y-word-ies. . . ."

But mostly, The Met Life is about choosing between golden oak or bird's-eye maple for the kids' rooms. The magazine is filled with photographs of people between twenty-five and forty-five living in city homes filled with straw, wicker, natural wood and canned kumquats. One couple describes their home as a "work in progress." Rooms and furniture are described as "witty." We hear about movers and shakers like "vegetable visionary" Frieda Kaplan, the woman who gave us yellow watermelon.

Meanwhile, in Macy's basement—aka The Cellar at Macy's-on-the-Square—the man who first slapped a nasturtium on a salad is holding up his gravlax. The audience applauds. Jeremiah Tower, the Laurence Olivier of chefs (he even resembles the great actor), has just performed the culinary equivalent of Hamlet's soliloquy.

Women in "Living The Met Life" aprons walk down the aisles giving us samples of the gravlax to taste. It slides right down, like salmon Jell-O.

When the demo is over, I ask Jeremiah Tower, "Why are you doing this?"

He says, "Because I believe in Macy's."

And, you know, I believe Jeremiah Tower believes in Macy's.

I believe Jeremiah can make bucks off Macy's and Macy's can make bucks off Jeremiah. You scratch my lox and I'll scratch yours.

I believe *Metropolitan Home* can make bucks off everyone between twenty-five and forty-five who lives in the city but would like to believe it's the country.

But I'm not sure what I believe in. I'm still in the midst of becoming rather than being.

Where Have All the
G Spots Gone?

You remember the G spot, an anatomical discovery that was greeted by women's magazines with as much enthusiasm as physicists embracing nuclear fission. The spot's existence aroused national attention five years ago.

It was five years exactly. I know because I learned of its existence during my daughter's third-birthday party. A number of beer-drinking dads at the party kept rushing to the room where I had left one of my favorite journals, *Sexual Medicine Today*.

An article in the journal—entitled "Developments in Sexual Research: Female Ejaculation Documented"—contained a comment that caught everyone's eye: "Although researchers still don't understand the mechanism, they have found that stimulation of the Grafenberg spot—the once-disputed erogenous zone in the vagina which has now been documented in over 400 women—can cause ejaculation."

This information, popularized in a best-selling book, set off a veritable Vesuvius of anatomical curiosity. I was one of the curious, for personal as well as scientific reasons. It seems the author of the book was a woman with two-thirds the same name as mine, one Alice Kahn Ladas.

As a result, people began to confuse the two of us. At cocktail parties, when I would introduce myself as a writer, I would invariably be subjected to a knowing wink and a comment like, "G-spot lady! You free tonight?"

You must remember that five years ago was a peak time in the paperback sexual revolution, an era when we not only accepted the idea that women should experience orgasm but expected that the orgasms had gosh-darned better be whoppers. Numerous books appeared guiding women to the best, the most complete, the total and even—something men could only dream about— the multiple. It seems only natural that all this resulted in the current love-too-much backlash.

Another result is that the "once-disputed" spot is being disputed again. Research published in a recent issue of the *Journal of Sex and Marriage Therapy* by Heli Alzate, a professor of sexology in Colombia, and Zwi Hoch, a physician in Israel (think of their phone bills!), concludes "Evidence in support of the G spot . . . is *so* far inconclusive."

Alice Kahn Ladas was only two-thirds right. In short: Maybe we got it, maybe we don't and maybe only some of us got it.

Furthermore, Alzate and Hoch—or Heli and Zwi, as I like to think of them—comment that "the extensive publicity given to the so-called 'female ejaculation' in the book by Alice Kahn Ladas, et al., is unwarranted." Since publicity can never be undone, the most we can hope for is a public service message: "Attention, women of the world. Abandon your search. The G Spot is located five centimeters south of Never-Never-Land."

Most of Heli and Zwi's quarrel has to do with the sensational language that entered the "Does G Exist?" debate. In particular, they object to use of analogues like "female ejaculation," "female penis" and "female scrotum." They go so far as to cite in their scientific paper a book by literary critic I. A. Richards on *The Meaning of Meaning*.

And they are certainly right. It is linguistic sexism of the rankest kind. Nobody, for example, would think of calling a nose the "male breast."

But the real point of their research, which drew scientists out of the woodwork from Bogotá to Haifa, is that all the publicity about the G spot led to an unprecedented epidemic of female sexual inadequacy. "Although allaying the fears of 'abnormality' among the few true ejaculators," the authors conclude, putting the G spot in the spotlight "may generate frustration and performance anxiety among the majority of women."

Thank you, doctors. It had to be said. Forget your G spot and just get happy.

We live in such unstable times. The words "in" and "out" are used more frequently than "true" and "false." Now the G spot has gone the way of the Hula Hoop and the mesquite hibachi. One day it's the "in" anatomical feature, the next it's out, out, damn spot.

But this trend slave is bothered by one little thought. I can understand the ephemeral nature of fads in fashion, in household items, in automobiles. But you'd think an anatomical part would have a little more staying power. Our bodies are now changing as much as our selves.

Thanks to Alice Kahn Ladas, millions of women searched for spots like desperate bargain seekers at a White Flower Day sale. No one wanted to come out without one.

What could be more a sign of the times than an anatomy fad? It's the ultimate answer to the question: What's hot and what's not?

Bathroom Lib

If you're a woman—and who isn't these days?—you know where the real fight for equality and justice is taking place. The struggle is not in the boardrooms but in the bathrooms of America, not at the door of the men's club but at the door of the men's room. The Rev. Jerry Falwell recognized the gravity of the situation when he said, "God intended Adam and Eve, not Adam and Steve. Next thing you know there'll be unisex toilets."

Unisex toilets: the ultimate sign of moral decay . . . or an idea whose time has come?

The impetus behind this in-depth look at bathroom liberation begins with a long line of anxious women standing outside the women's room. Meanwhile, men blithely pop in and out of the men's room, each leaving with a look of smug relief on his face.

Finally, one long-standing suffragette breaks from the pack. She's mad as hell and she's not going to take it anymore. Plus—she's gotta go! Into the men's room she marches like the Allies entering occupied Paris.

What kind of woman would defy the social contract that says men in Men's and women in Women's? (Or, in the case of certain seafood joints, men in Buoys and women in Gulls?)

The typical bathroom liberator is an attractive woman between twenty-five and forty-five with at least a college education and possibly an advanced degree in the social sciences. In fact, she is a woman very much like myself. In fact, she has, at times, been myself.

It's a scene familiar to any woman. You are at a play or a concert or a conference. Perhaps you have been on a long rowboat ride with water, water everywhere. In the worst scenario, you have had a drink or two. Waiting in the long line will result in either a physiological conquest or your most embarrassing moment. But to enter the empty men's room—that's one giant step for womankind.

I'll never forget my First Time. I had a whole story ready about how I'd recently flunked my vision test and mistook the M for a W. But no questions were asked. I came, I went, I flushed.

After that, I got cocky. Sometimes, if both rooms were empty, I'd use the men's room just for kicks. Like a terrorist, I'd leave my telltale lipstick-blotted tissues on the sink. The kiss-off of defiance.

As the handwriting on the stall indicates, a certain amount of reverse liberation has been taking place. Witness the following piece of latrinalia spotted in a women's room at Printers Inc., a Palo Alto bookstore: "The graffiti in the men's room is much better. A Man."

Unfortunately, just as I was learning to appreciate the men's room mural art of anatomical exaggeration, my career as the Cortez of the tidy bowl came to an abrupt halt. I entered what I believed to be an empty men's room only to meet the blank, doglike stare of— what else?—a man standing red-handed at the urinal.

Suddenly I knew my place—in line. That urinal was my Waterloo. But for every woman who throws in the towel, another joins the cause. Bathroom liberation has become a major frontier for millions of women who refuse to take things standing up.

At a recent all-day Jungian forum, a state of siege was

narrowly averted at the Palace of Fine Arts washrooms. The assembled Jungians had just seen a film in which an analyst explains that urination is genuine self-expression, the one urge you can't repress. During the break, a mob of women in a frenzy of unrepression invaded the less crowded men's room. Ushers were asked to stand guard so men could use the men's room. One man who attempted to enter was told by a woman standing by the door, "Get in line, bub."

Dr. John Boe, a scholar who wrote about the incident in the *San Francisco Jung Institute Library Journal*, said, "The women felt the men were interfering with their genuine self-expression, and the men felt the women were interfering with their genuine self-expression. And the fault was really in the architecture. . . ."

The question then is: Can the fault, dear brutes, be rectified by the unisex toilet?

Such major cultural changes require the support of politicians, architects and business people, as well as the ordinary toilet-using community. Are these crucial citizens ready to help turn the tide?

California Secretary of State March Fong Eu rose to power in an earlier era of bathroom liberation. But she doubts that unisex units can meet the demand for toilet justice.

The woman who freed the pay toilet—who once literally took a sledgehammer to a locked john at the state capitol while a band played "The Best Things in Life Are Free"—does not see herself as a men's-room liberator. In fact, Eu confesses, "I've never tried a unisex washroom."

Eu sees the urinal—that ceramic symbol of male freedom—as a barrier to bladder justice. "I'm fond of urinals," she said. "They're cleaner—a man might miss a toilet. But I can't see how a woman can use a urinal."

Perhaps Dr. Eu has never seen what women firefighters can do, what women athletes can do and what women bears can do in the woods.

I asked Dr. Muriel Friedman (one of only seven female board-certified urologists) how she accounted for the long lines outside women's rooms. Do women spend more time in the bathroom chatting and primping, or do they actually need to go more frequently?

She assured me that men and women have the same bladder capacity—450cc's. But she does note that "men have a healthier attitude toward urination. Women are more afraid of bathrooms, afraid to sit on toilets."

Furthermore, Dr. Friedman offers an insight into what potty power is all about: "A lot of women have a love/hate relationship with bathrooms."

But the fact remains, there are also a lot of women who'd love to go but hate to wait in line.

Midway Through the Battle of Mid-Life

Our long national nightmare is almost over. My mid-life crisis is over, and yours will be too, soon.

My crisis took only about fifteen years. The swift can whiz through it in about five. Average duration of crisis: ten years. That leaves you with only another ten or twenty years of well-adjusted mid-life to endure.

Mid-life begins around thirty-something and ends around sixty-something. The good news is, if you stay in crisis for fifteen years, the ordeal is half over before you have to spend the remaining years cowering in pathetic acceptance.

Those attacked by premature baldness or early wrinkles may be plunged into a more serious form of the crisis known as Mid-Life Panic. This can lead to compulsive overexercise, compulsive nonselective sex and compulsive hoarding of Rogaine and Retin-A. Others are allowed the luxury of a soft landing, realizing slowly but surely that the cup isn't half empty—it's evaporating!

The mid-life crisis usually begins with a checkup at the doctor's. You feel you are in perfect health. And you are. It's just that you suddenly realize the doctor is some punk kid. The fact that the doctor is younger than you makes you sick. You can no longer call him Dr. Silverstein. Instead, you say, "Do you know a damn thing about systemic yeast, Sean?"

Then you consult a lawyer. It's time to make out your will. Or maybe you have a book contract. Or maybe you want to put out a contract on your noisy neighbor. You enter the doors of Sharkey, Sharkey and Goniff. "Mr. Goniff will see you now," the receptionist says.

There, behind the large desk and in front of those great big books, is a twenty-eight-year-old boy in a fancy suit and a paisley tie with a matching handkerchief and, perhaps, if you'd mentally undress him, a matching paisley diaper. "How can we help you, ma'am," he asks.

"I just wanted to know if mid-life crisis is a valid defense against Murder One," you ask as you take out Mr. AK and Mr. 47. Standing over his body, you say, "Never call me 'ma'am' again."

Mid-life is a time to reflect on all those young years of fighting. Years of wanting dignity, respect. Don't treat me like a child! Don't treat me like a girl! Don't treat me like a—gulp—sex object!

But how come I still remember that it was exactly six years ago today when I was walking down Mission Street in my new red blouse and a guy said, "Hey, mama. You want to have my baby?" How come I suddenly want someone to treat me like a sex object—just one more time?

Maybe we have a hard time with mid-life because of our basic prejudice against the middle of things. Monkey in the Middle is a game about a jerk in the middle trying to steal the ball. Middle class is often synonymous with conformity, boredom and lack of imagination. We want the first piece of cake, the head of the class, the end of the rainbow, a house on the Coast.

The problem is not so much that we're old but that we're no longer young. We were "the kids" for so long. We grew up with the worst attitudes toward aging of any generation in history. We were always going to be James Dean. We never wanted to be Jim Backus.

Look at the dramas of middle age. Will I lose my job? Can I stand my job? Will I have enough for the mortgage payment? Will I be able to get a week in Kauai? Can I get my bike up this hill? Can I keep up with myself?

I listen to Tracy Chapman's "Fast Car," a song about a teenager dreaming of blowing her dreary life and going Somewhere. Then I think about when I was fifteen and heard Maria singing "Somewhere" to Tony.

Well, I got in the fast car twenty-five years ago, and it slowly led here. Somewhere. Now all I'm supposed to do is make sure that car doesn't break down.

Finally, I understand what makes some fool leave a perfectly good job, divorce a wonderful spouse or sell a house with a 7 percent mortgage. But if you weather the storm, you can hold on to all these things and still ride off into that condo at Sunset Village.

You know—pack up your troubles in your new white Porsche and smile, smile, smile.

Cher Gives Us a Nose Job

Why do we want to smell like Cher? That was the question in my mind as I stood crushed in with four thousand others sharing the new art form: celebrity department-store visits. Forget Godot. We were waiting for Cher.

And standing there in such close proximity to the great masses of humanity, I could not help but wonder why we would want to smell like any person.

In all the hype surrounding the unleashing of Uninhibited by Cher—in all the media stories about how Cher (despite her navel uniforms) really is inhibited, about how Cher survived those dark days when Sonny wouldn't let her wear perfume—we have overlooked the profound nature of what's going down here. Is there not some cultural meaning in the cult of celebrity odors?

I could understand wanting Cher's looks, Cher's job, Cher's agent. Cher's little boyfriend ain't bad, either. We have all heard of the "sweet smell of success," but who is to say Cher has bottled it?

There is the obvious explanation: None of us want to smell like ourselves. John Cleese, the master of embarrassing humor, exploited this fact in *A Fish Called Wanda* as he showed characters constantly sniffing their own socks, underarms, etc. We live in a world in which smelling like ourselves is a sign of failure.

As I found myself between a costume-jewelry counter

and a hard place, I was amazed at what a range of people want to smell like Cher. In the crowd were businessmen in sincere suits, grandes dames with blue-rinsed hair, young guys in earrings, no-nonsense businesswomen in No Nonsense panty hose, Medusa-headed Cher wannabes, preppie boys, mothers with babes in arms, the rainbow coalition of multiethnic America, all shouting "We want Cher!" Could it simply be that stupidity knows no boundary?

The two security guys keeping the aisle clear next to where I stood fended off an encyclopedia of lame excuses as people tried to get up front, within smelling range of Her Cherness. "I'm with the press. . . . I'm with Cher's entourage. . . . I just want to go shopping. . . . I MUST get through. . . ." Only the lady who threw up and three others who threatened to faint were allowed through the security line.

Cher, by now twenty minutes late, was nowhere to be sniffed. But the announcer reminded us we could watch her videos on the numerous monitors set up around the store "for your convenience and for a live simulcast when Cher appears." The crowd began to boo menacingly.

Just then a stylish woman came by with a spray bottle of Uninhibited by Cher and zappped me on the wrist. Was this a new form of crowd control? One squeeze puts your mind at ease.

I thrust my wrist at the security guard, feeling that forty-five minutes of sharing our Cher space had bonded us for life. "Does that smell like Cher?" I asked him. "Smells like vanilla," he said.

A fellow sharer of our little corner of the display case, a handsome man wearing a T-shirt with a quote from Balzac, took the liberty of sniffing my wrist. "It smells more like Sonny," he said.

Suddenly the cameras began flashing like strobe

lights. Cher was in the room. From where I stood, you couldn't smell her, you couldn't see her, but she walked with us and she talked with us.

For twenty minutes Cher dialogued the crowd—a half-obscene, semiliterate tease and comedy act that told me one thing. Cher is an idol because she is the kind of take-no-prisoners lady who would never spend an hour in a dangerously crowded department store to get a whiff of Cher. As she said so profoundly when she walked out and saw the mob, "In the best of all possible worlds, this really sucks."

If there's a sucker born willing to pay to smell like Cher—it ain't her, babe. But those who lead quiet lives reeking of desperation will go to great lengths for some link to greatness. Even one that vaporizes and costs $175 an ounce.

Life's Little
Cardless Moments

You're having a special moment, but it's not a Kodak moment. It's time to relax, but it's not Miller Time. You wouldn't really rather have a Buick. It's a nongreeting-card occasion.

You look through the categories at the stationery shop—Birthday . . . Humorous Birthday . . . Get Well . . . Wedding . . . Bereavement . . . Humorous Bereavement—but there is no category for what you need.

My husband and I had one of those moments. I've known him since we were sophomoric high school sophomores. "You know, honey," I said to him, "we're almost the age our parents were when we first met each other."

"Oh boy," he said. "I think we should send each other greeting cards on this one."

(Actually, I didn't say "honey." My husband and I use "honey" only sarcastically, as in, "Your turn to apply the Tidy Bowl, honey.")

Sure enough, there is no Old as Your Parents Were section between Sweet Sixteen and Silver Anniversary. There's not a single card saying: "To My Husband, We're Growing Old, Fat and Ugly Together."

Here's another nongreeting-card moment. Recently, I had a friend who was falsely accused and eventually exonerated on charges of child molestation. He is a wonderful person, and his life was turned into hell for seven months because of one misinformed or stupid or evil person. To help him through his ordeal, his friends organized a chain of support. We would each leave a gift on his doorstep every morning until the trial. I went into the store and looked at the cards. Not a single one said, "Congratulations! You've Been Falsely Accused of Child Molestation!"

Obviously, Hallmark is not keeping up with the times.

A final example arises from a conversation I overheard between two men leaving work for lunch. One was saying he wanted to go down to a certain outdoor plaza where women office workers are known to congregate at lunchtime. He said he wanted to check them out but was afraid his wife would get mad.

"Well, that's ridiculous," said the friend. "Tell your wife that just because you're married, that doesn't mean you're dead."

"Yeah," said the married man, encouraged. "I'll tell her, 'Just because I take a test ride, that doesn't mean I'll buy the car.' "

"NO! Test ride is not the concept here!" explained his friend.

"I guess you're right," said the married man. "I suppose I should say, 'Just because I go into the showroom, that doesn't mean I want to buy the car.' "

"Much better," said his friend, as they both headed for the Plaza de las Administrative Assistants.

Now, if some sharp greeting-card company were on its toes, this poor slob wouldn't have had to invent his own inadequate metaphors. One crummy phrase could wreck an entire marriage. The poor couple would never have lived to see each other get as old as their parents were when they first met.

And if greeting cards were really keeping pace with our evolving world, the husband could have gone into a card shop and bought: "To My Wife, Thinking of Having an Affair but Want You to Think I'm Just Planning to Trade In the Volvo, Honey."

Finding That Special
Psychotherapeutic Someone

It's hardest to find when you need it most. It's one of the most important relationships in your life. It involves commitment to another person. Yet you cannot just trust your heart to a perfect stranger.

So how do you choose a therapist?

The experienced therapy consumer will have no problem. The experienced therapy consumer will already have gone through six or seven different therapists by the age of forty. But what of the beginner, the psycho-virgin, the babe in the analytic woods?

Choosing a therapist would be so much easier if newspapers would start a therapy personals section. Then we might see ads like:

• Well-read, well-educated professor at Ivy League college with own home, sports car and emotional baggage seeks classic Freudian.

• Woman who loves too much seeks handsome, married hypnotherapist. No head trips, please.

• Hip, athletic, urban male into obsessive-compulsive disorder wants Jungian play therapist for quiet evenings.

• Environmentally sensitive lesbian seeks radical-feminist, neo-Reichian neurolinguistic programmer.

But newspapers are no help when it comes to finding therapists. Unlike a book or a movie, therapists don't get reviewed. "A session with Dr. Lobestein is like a jog in the Bois de Boulogne. . . ." says *The New York Times*. The *Kansas City Star* says, "Don't miss the part where he asks, 'When were you first aware of the dragon?'" *Consumer Reports* says, "At $45 a pop, his free associations are a steal." Siskel and Ebert say, "A genius with regression. Two thumbs aren't enough."

But there isn't even a stinkin' *New York Review of Shrinks* right there in the therapy capital of America. The best way to find a therapist is to get a recommendation from a friend. But it's hard to feel totally convinced when someone says, "This guy is great. I've been seeing him three times a week for ten years."

Another problem with finding a therapist is coming up with one who will see you when you are actually disturbed. For some reason, most therapists want to see only people who are articulate, cheerful and working at a well-paying job. Many deal only with the walking wounded and seem repulsed by actual mental illness.

I had a friend who got through one and a half paid sessions with a therapist. In the middle of the second session, after she covered her parents' deaths and the fire that destroyed everything and just as she was getting to her suicide attempt, the therapist suddenly stopped her and said, "I'm sorry. I should tell you that I don't see depressives."

True story.

There are community groups that have a referral service for those seeking psychotherapy. You can look through the files and see things like: No schizophrenics, please. . . . Alcoholics need not apply. . . . Delusions of grandeur not welcome. . . . Women only.

God forbid an actual psychopath should ever want to take the cure.

It's important that when you see a therapist for the first time, you take the initiative and interview her. Although she will mislabel you an aggressive personality, you must find out if you have come to a full-service station.

The first question you will want to ask is "Do you validate?" Validation is the biggest thing in therapy since giving permission. It means that they will let you be you. Strange as it may sound, a lot of people need to pay to get things they should have got from their parents or a parking lot attendant.

Finally, you will want to know what kind of support your therapist has to offer. Therapists vary like panty hose on the support issue. You need to know right away if you are dealing with firm support, mild support or control top.

Remember, if you can keep your head while all about you are losing theirs and blaming it on you, you should have no problem finding a shrink. It's the one true test of sanity.

I Saw London,
I Saw France

Let me tell you about my underpants.

I have just had a complete underwear makeover. It's part of a story that began when I was a teenager.

My mama sold underwear. Someday I will tell my children about how their grandma walked two miles in the snow every day to sell underwear.

On her days off, Mama used to buy me underwear. Not just any old underwear either. Red lace on Valentine's Day. Black lace for my birthday. White lace for spring. I was embarrassed to get undressed around the other kids.

When I was in college, I would get CARE packages from home just like the other girls. While theirs would contain chocolate chip cookies, mine would hold six bras and half-slips in assorted colors.

When my mother died ten years ago, I had to buy myself underwear for the first time in my life. Anyone who thinks this is a simple task has never entered the arcane world of ladies' lingerie.

There are one-piece, two-piece, three-piece under-suits. There are things that squeeze you in and things that push you out. There are garments that seem to do nothing but, like Emerson's Rhodora, remind you that "beauty is its own excuse for being."

There are straps and snaps and elastic slingshots.

There are hooks on bras that only a mechanical engineering professor could love.

You try these items on, but who can tell if they fit? What is their purpose? Hygiene? To hide your shame? To serve you up like a harem girl or to create a slick Spandex sea lion whose dress slides down like a wave toward the pebbled shore?

For ten years I have been a lingerie agnostic, believing there could be some purpose to it all but not knowing what. Furtively, I would rush into stores and pick up the most conservative and cheapest of the basic garments, knowing no more about exotic items like a teddy or a *bustier* than I do about a chador.

Then I met Peggy Bryant, Emporium-Capwell's Underwear Engineer 1. ("Saleslady" doesn't even begin to hint at it.) Part psychologist, part aesthetician, part mechanic, Peggy was my guide to the underworld of underwear. She led me through the trauma, the straps, the bizarre front snaps, to be born again in washable nylon tricot.

Like others who minister to the needy, she was *there* for me. Doctors see patients lying down naked screaming, "Is it cancer?" and psychologists see clients sitting up sobbing, "Am I nuts?" Peggy Bryant sees grown women buckled in lace and elastic asking, "How do I look?"

"That looks good," says Peggy simply and earnestly, as she gently adjusts your womanhood so that the cups don't runneth over.

"I'd take the larger ones," she says without judgment, handing you the underpants that leave no dreaded panty line. Then she allows you a few minutes alone in the dressing room. Time enough to dance around and sing "I Feel Pretty."

But on the way home, I break into a sweat. Thirty-five dollars for the clothes no one sees!

I think biblical thoughts about the evils of vanity. I think about what I could have bought. Dinner at Chez Swanko. A teeth cleaning and set of X rays. A new *Remembrance of Things Past*.

I hear a voice on the radio say, ". . . And for only thirty-five dollars a year, you can clothe, feed and sustain one of these children."

Then I think of Mama and of Peggy Bryant and of all the women through all of time who only stood and waited. Their efforts were not in vain. They found a garment and filled it.

Sex So Safe You'll Never Want It Again

Sex. It's no longer a subject to be treated with kid gloves. It's a subject to be treated with latex rubber gloves. And a latex rubber dental dam. And a synthetic fiber condom.

Soon the ideal playmate will be wearing a Three Mile Island yellow rubber antinuclear suit.

Safe sex is like the weather. Everyone talks about it, but until recently hardly anyone has gotten down to specifics. Now health centers across the country are distributing explicit safe-sex information, and the assumptions about common sexual practices contained in these guidelines amount to a virtual Kinsey Report.

Recently, a copy of the X-rated publication *Planning for Health*, put out by the Kaiser Foundation Health Plan, fell into my hot little hands. Don't be fooled by the photo on the cover of the two sweet old ladies playing Trivial Pursuit. The safe-sex guidelines are a stunner.

Kaiser is to be congratulated for spelling things out. For a health organization to do otherwise in the face of a deadly epidemic would be gross irresponsibility. Still, safety is not a hot item in sexual fantasyland. As Freud might put it: Za libido ain't lookin' for safety.

Let's face it: One person's safe sex is another's abstinence. If I learned anything in my fifteen-year career as a nurse it was this: "When it comes to sex, never assume." My first job as a nurse was in a county family-planning clinic. The doctors wrote birth control prescriptions that we nurses filled from the clinic dispensary. If a woman chose condoms as her method of birth control, the doctor would write: "Rx—one month's supply of condoms." One day I discovered that while I was shoveling packets of Trojans into shopping bags, Carmelita, a sixty-year-old co-worker, was dispensing a three-pack to cover the same prescription.

In the article entitled "Better Safe Than Sorry," guidelines are offered to *everyone* who has had non-monogamous sex since 1978. That's right, Jim Bakker, this means you. Those fifteen minutes in a motel room just cost you a fortune in rubber gloves.

The article quotes gynecologist Dr. Arthur Levit as saying, "If you know *with absolute certainty* that both you and your partner have been in a monogamous relationship since 1978 and that neither of you would be considered high-risk for any other reason (for example, receiving blood products prior to 1985 or using intravenous drugs), then you may not have to follow these practices. But everyone else should."

Everyone else! It's like *Revenge of the Nerds*. Those people who've had a mundane sex life are suddenly rewarded with no-holds-barred party-time; while the wild and crazy set are stuck in Three Mile Island jumpsuits for the rest of eternity.

The guidelines divide sexual activities into Safe, Possibly Safe and Unsafe. Now, I thought I'd heard of everything in my career as a nurse. To be honest, I have removed mangos from places where the mango don't shine. Still, there were a few phrases here that caught my eye.

Possibly Safe are "water sports." (Their quotes. I'd have used exclamation points as they do in Spanish.)

100 – ALICE KAHN

You can call Kaiser to find out what this means, but I'll tell you it has nothing to do with scuba diving or wind-surfing.

Marcy Kates, editor of the publication, said they had to eliminate the phrase "water sports" from a later edition after several readers thought it meant swimming, "rather than what goes on in a Harold Robbins novel."

Also Possibly Safe is cunnilingus (look it up, kids) with a rubber dental dam. Kaiser pharmacy is stocking this item, and the requests are pouring in. Anyone who has had root-canal work will recall this stimulating sexual aid.

Definitely Not Safe is "sharing sex toys." Now, why do I have the feeling they're not talking about teddy bears?

So what is absolutely, certainly, guaranteed safe sex? Massage, hugging, body-to-body rubbing (there are more colorful euphemisms for this), "social" kissing (as opposed to what those antisocial French frogs do), masturbation and fantasy.

Which proves one thing: We should have quit in junior high.

Mondo Bizarro Scientifique

"Why not a patented mouse?" I thought to myself as I wandered through a field of frost-free strawberries.

Another great idea would be a cross between a frost-free strawberry and a patented mouse. This would create both a frost-free mouse and a walkaway shortcake.

I tried calling my friend Marge to tell her this idea. Marge is into R&D. But my phone lost its memory and I couldn't reach her.

So I lit up a smoke-free cigarette and went to the toning and tanning salon. One machine passively created my bicep while another turned it a nice honey beige.

I put on my earphones and headed home. That's when I thought of a solution to the walking-wounded problem. What we do is issue earphones to all the people talking to themselves. No radios. Just the earphones. Then they'll look like nice normal people singing along with Sting.

When I got home, I started to make dinner but the microwave was down, so instead of taking three minutes, the lasagna won't be ready until next Tuesday at ten o'clock. I programmed the VCR to start recording "Thirty-something" in case I miss a new episode when the lasagna's done.

I pointed the remote at the radio and heard about a

scandal in the food technology business. A leading scientist got drunk, and they had to recall all the aloe vera potato chips. But the cool ranch shampoo and Cajun spice conditioner were selling briskly.

I zapped the radio with my new all-purpose remote, but I accidentally zapped the kids, too. It's a little like freeze tag. I left them on PAUSE while I watched a tape of yesterday's "Evening News."

Dan Rather said that scientists at Harvard announced a major breakthrough. While trying to understand the origin of life, they actually created a new mutant creature. It was half Sylvester Stallone and half jackass. You couldn't tell which end was up, but they both said "Yo."

I fast-forwarded the kids and put them to bed. The youngest kept screaming for grapes, her favorite bedtime snack. I was all out, so I rubbed a little Retin-A on some raisins and slipped them to her. They might taste weird, but it'll keep them from singing and dancing.

It was a beautiful night. There was a full moon, and it got me thinking about how no one goes to the moon anymore. I poured a glass of Tang and went out on the patio. The crickets were chirping like crazy, so I turned on the bug light, hoping they'd shut up.

I vowed that the next morning I was going to start a self-improvement program. Elizabeth Taylor's kind of my idol in that regard. She stopped using drugs. She took off all that weight. She even got that monkey off her chest.

Let him go back to writing for *Forbes*.

Sometimes I think the world is just the most wonderful place. I'm so happy to be living in the here and now. Just think, a hundred years ago I might have been working in a field. Two hundred years ago I might have been dead by the time I was thirty-five. Three hundred years ago I might have been burned as a witch just for thinking that women shouldn't have to do dishes.

I fell asleep and dreamed they had invented a mouse that could cure cancer. But I awoke at three in the morning with my heart pounding. Goldfish food! I forgot to buy goldfish food! You'd think by now they'd have self-feeding goldfish.

That's the real trouble with science today. It's so impractical.

Power Drinking

The singles scene is booming in the bars these days. The scene isn't dating but drinking, and the singles are the delicate, oak-aged barley of single-malt scotch. The market for this trendy liquor has grown 80 percent in the past six years.

With the single-malt scotch becoming as much a symbol of the eighties as phone machines and workout wear, I wondered why more women had not tried "a bonnie wee bit of the sweetie." So I decided to invite four women I knew out for a night of scotch treat, to answer that age-old question: What happens when real women drink scotch?

I was already a veteran of a coed scotch tasting. It started out with perfect dignity. Eric Schroeder, a University of California at Davis lecturer in English literature, stood in front of a map of Scotland pointing out the Highlands, the Lowlands, Speyside and other legendary spots that are to scotch what Provence is to herbs and spices. Six couples sat around a dining-room table —ten glasses of unidentified whiskey before each participant. It was all very formal. Hands were raised. Questions were asked. Then the games began.

We had a checklist to record our impression of each of the whiskeys. My notes began with elaborate descriptions: "Whiskey A—a deeper amber with slightly smoky aroma, tasting sweet and delicious like cognac." By the time I got down to Whiskey E, the volume in the room had gone up several decibels. The map of Scotland was on the floor. And my descriptions had degenerated to "Smells like medicine, tastes yummy, and looks like just plain piss."

What we had forgotten as we approached an educational evening of Glenfarclas and Laphroaig and Macallan was that the stuff was 86 to 104 proof and gets you quite bombed.

I kept this in mind as Toni, Arlyce, Judy and Egedia, and I met at the local yuppie bar, a place that lists its "liquor consultant" and twenty single-malt scotch whiskeys on the menu. Surrounded by mauve walls, lush plants, track lighting, spectacular waterfront views and a mob of men and women under fifty, we began our task —a serious evening of power drinking.

We ranged in age from twenty-seven to forty-three and a half (but who's counting?); our careers varied from newspaper columnist to real estate wheeler-dealer; and among us we had had ten kids, nine cars and seven husbands. It is, perhaps, statistically significant that we all had eaten light dinners of mashed or baked potatoes that evening. Do men, I wondered, ever suffer from this fear of barfing?

I turned on my tape recorder, knowing that note-taking would soon be compromised by my scotch-drinking prowess. Later, when I listened to the scotch tapes, one thing became clear: The stuff is truth serum. Perhaps it doesn't affect men that way. But how else can you explain that halfway through the night, after cognac-like Macallan and the less interesting Cardhu, four women who were practically strangers an hour earlier were exchanging stories about their first sexual encounter?

Our evening began innocently enough, with a discussion of our children's sex lives. Egedia told of her four-year-old-son Geno's engagement to Gabriella, a girl at nursery school. Judy and Arlyce, mothers of female teenagers, discussed the pros and cons of permitting youthful liaisons in the home. Then The Macallan and the sushi arrived.

I love a drink that takes an article and tastes like cognac. The twelve-year-old Macallan gives Mr. Rémy and Mr. Martin a run for their money. Unfortunately, the twenty-five-year-old Macallan, even at ten dollars a hit, was sold out.

After a brief discussion of the medical legends about scotch (a cure for constipation, a treatment for sore throats), we were feeling no pain. One of our group began describing her overprotected childhood, during which she was not allowed to date. But she demurely shared with us the fact that at thirteen she began having sex with a neighbor boy every day in the basement. Holding the tiny snifter of scotch, she smiled and said, "Of course, I still couldn't date."

Soon we were comparing first-time stories. Ages fifteen, seventeen, nineteen and nineteen respectively. "Any nineteen-year-old scotch?" Judy asked the waitress.

Toni reluctantly admitted that she was enjoying herself although she remained a scotch skeptic. "I hate this; it tastes like medicine," she said. "It's delicious," I insisted. However, I did look enviously over at the women at the next table drinking their margaritas. You don't get little umbrellas on your whiskey glass.

We moved on to Cardhu, which the waitress told us was a favorite at the single-malt bar. We liked it least.

Halfway into the round of Cardhu and Cajun shrimp, Judy told the story of the teacher at her child's nursery school, who asked, "Are you into open marriage? I'm crazy about your husband." We all drank to the harpy's ultimate demise.

By the time round three rolled around, we were becoming old friends. "You know," announced Toni, "this is a momentous occasion because we all currently have husbands. What are the historic odds of that ever happening again?"

To celebrate we each got a different scotch and shared burnt cream and praline pecan ice cream. (I had read that Hugh Mitcalfe, marketing director for The Macallan, takes his whiskey with ice cream.) We ordered a Mortlach (too strong), a Talisker (smoky), a Glenlivet (loved it), a Glenfarclas (fiery) and a Glenfiddich (smooth). "We've got a Glen fetish," Arlyce told the waitress.

Arlyce said her favorite drink was Courvoisier, although she also loved bourbon, which her southern aristocrat first mother-in-law taught her to appreciate. I noticed that our reasons for liking certain liquors had more to do with the context than taste.

I said I liked martinis just because of the shape of the glass. Judy said her favorite is a margarita because of the chopped ice.

"Mine too," said Egedia. "It's like a Slurpee. I don't think that women are quite ready to drink scotch. They want a drink with more volume, one that they can nurse."

"That's the problem here," suggested Toni. "It's over too fast. Is there a sexual connotation?"

"Women want a slow hand," added Egedia. "However, if you're going out with someone you hardly know and you're going to bed with him you definitely need one of these."

"And a condom," I reminded her.

"This is very smooth," said Toni, admiring the Glen-fiddich. "But it still smells like scotch."

"Then don't smell it," I suggested. "What's your favorite drink anyway?"

"Bud Light," she answered. "Actually, I don't like liquor. I was raised in a bar that my dad owned. It was pitch dark at twelve noon, like going into an opium den. But people come here to look at each other. This is not a bar, it's a scene."

Most of us were raised on nightmare movies about women drunks. The classic was *I'll Cry Tomorrow*, the Susan Hayward melodrama about the life of actress and alcoholic Lillian Roth.

We all agreed that it was this perception of drinking whiskey which alienated us from the foreboding bar and its sleazy ambience. Which is precisely why I think we'll see more women sipping single malts at mauve and white yuppitoriums like the one we were at. It's a whole new context, a new experience. A total escape from the careers and men and kids that dominate our lives. This was Door Number Three.

We didn't have a guilty drink at a darkened bar. We made the scene. We had group therapy. We enjoyed sharing our deepest secrets and getting silly. Definitely an idea for the stressful eighties: a women's consciousness-lowering session.

The Temple of Lifestyle

I am in the inner sanctum of lifestyle—the photography screening room of *New York* magazine. On the boards are several sexy poses of a veal roast. Standing over them is my childhood friend Jordan Schaps, photography director of the magazine. In a town where everyone is an armchair interior decorator, Jordan is a Master of the Taste Universe.

"This is to die for," says Jordan, selecting the exact view of veal that will be *New York*'s Playmate of the Month. Around him, several assistants—all young, all gorgeous, all sporting very blunt haircuts, very black clothes and very silver jewelry—bring in more potential centerfolds. One holds up a photograph of waffles with a jalapeño soufflé, which is, according to Jordan, "to drop dead for."

Whether he is showcasing food, fashion or political figures, Jordan is totally aware of the power of his decisions. After a special issue on interiors, a man reported that several customers came to his antique shop, held up photos from *New York* magazine and said, "I want this." An interior decorator told him about the blank check he received from a newly rich couple who said, "Just give us an apartment like in *New York* magazine."

Once upon a whim, Jordan decided to photograph penguin statuettes for an issue on Christmas gift ideas.

Two weeks later, the New York Folk Art Museum phoned him to say they had sold six hundred sets of folk-art penguins to devotees of *New York* style.

In a cruel twist of one-ins-manship, *New York*'s restaurant critic, Gael Greene, did a piece on "Scenes," places so "in" you have to know somebody or actually be somebody just to walk in the door. The piece concluded with a description of a club called "Drex," described as another "triumph" of clubmaster Peppo Urbanowitz.

Wrote Greene: "The phone is unlisted. No one knows the actual address. Just watch for a blindfolded doorman behind a teal-blue rope somewhere on West Street. He is flanked by two mute mutants. Once you establish your credentials, you are blindfolded too. . . ." Inside Drex, the critic warned, "Don't trip over Bianca" and "Don't miss the fruit-salad pizza."

Of course, Jordan, like others on the magazine's staff, got calls from people begging for help to get into Drex.

Perhaps, Jordan's biggest photography "scoop," the lifestyle junkies' equivalent of entering King Tut's tomb or Al Capone's vault, was when Jordan photographed the bedroom of *New Yorker* editor Bob Gottlieb. Unlike Geraldo, he didn't come out with nothing but his mike in his hand. Jordan was the man who discovered that Gottlieb had his bedroom walls lined with bookshelves filled with the world's largest collection of plastic handbags.

As I write about Jordan, it is not hard for me to believe he has succeeded, but I am awed that he has surmounted the Straight Face Obstacle. When I think back to our time running together as teenagers, I remember him as someone so outrageous, so funny, that it was impossible to take anything seriously when you were with him. It is even hard for me to say his name, since I spent my adolescence calling him by a nickname closer to Stinky or Butch.

Especially, I remember Jordan at the gathering after my father's funeral, greeting guests at the door like a Catskills MC. When a particularly stuffy aunt showed up, he said, "May I take your mink?" Then he proceeded to walk over to the windows and begin scrubbing them with her full-length black Balenciaga.

Although Jordan says he hates to go out in Manhattan on weekends because the streets are crowded with "OBs" (people from the Outer Boroughs), he took me to one of those incredibly "in" new restaurants, Rakel's— that's R-A-K-E-L.

Like a fool, I listened to him when he said it was a casual place. Everyone in the joint except us was dressed to the nines. But because Jordan Schaps is Mr. Lifestyle, the chef kept sending us more plates of food to die for. Raw salmon shaped like Madame Butterfly. A tiny pancake contoured exactly like the moon. A lobster taken from its shell and reshaped so that to me it resembled the statue of Napoleon in the Place Vendôme. Crab cakes floating in colored sauces patterned after the chef's favorite Mondrian.

But we were acting obnoxious. We were giggling like teenagers. We were back in Woolworth's eating banana splits. And when the elegant, anorexic fashion model at the next table shot us a drop-dead look, I fully expected Jordan to start wiping the floors with her faux-leopard coat.

When dessert came, I thought we'd died and gone to lifestyle heaven. We had our *gâteau* and ate it too.

Little Myth Female

Yesterday (or was it last week?) I was in my high-toned neighborhood bookstore attempting to complete a purchase. Buying things may be easy for you, but for me it requires a commitment to what I'm buying, acceptance of the cost burden and evaluation of the statement I'm making.

And, of course, I have to worry about whether God will punish me for coveting worldly goods.

After several months of careful consideration, I had decided the time was right to move forward on the acquisition of *The Fractal Geometry of Nature* by Mandelbrot (not to be confused with the Jewish pastry of the same name). Since the decision involved the commitment of thirty-five smackers, I had to put in several hours devising a reasonable payment plan.

First, I attempted to gain credit, which can be done in this bookstore by selling used books. I offered up my entire collection of movie-star bio first editions. But picky, picky, picky—they didn't take one. The rejection of *Shelley, Also Known as Shirley*, the true story of Shelley Winters, was a particularly painful blow to my good taste.

The deep snobbism of these culture peddlers was revealed with the reaction to my next offer. After much agonizing, I presented my rare assortment of calorie counters—spanning nearly three decades and sixty pounds. I even included an out-of-print 1959 Dell Purse Book containing a dated Metropolitan Life "What You Should Weigh" table, which is of significant antiquarian value.

But this will teach me to cast my pearls before swine —not a single calorie counter counted.

Finally, desperate for the book but unwilling to actually cough up the cash for it, I brought in my never opened set of coffee-table art books. I've had little use for them since I switched to tea.

The scam worked. In exchange for what surely must be three hundred dollars in mint-condition unsellable art books, I got the thirty-five dollars in credit.

I had one final trick up my sleeve. I had heard that this particular store offered a discount to poor, suffering authors who are shameless enough to ask for it. Having recently been catapulted into the middle class myself, I hesitated to be so gauche. But after seeing a certain mansion-dwelling, Jag-driving, Armani-wearing novelist exercise the fiction of poverty, I thought: Grub for it!

Cleverly donning my shabbiest black turtleneck and old tweed jacket (but deciding the beret was definitely too obvious), I approached the counter and in a sweet little Twistian voice said, "May I have s'more discount, please."

To my astonishment, it worked. Were others to imitate my act, it could make shoplifting obsolete—no small feat in a town like Berkeley.

The book in hand, the terms agreed upon, two months of consumer strategizing were about to result in a purchasing coup. Then: devastation.

"You can't get a discount if you're paying with credit," the owner said. I could hardly believe what I was hearing. All was lost. Do I then pay with cash and save the credit—the very credit that I had struggled and sacrificed and compromised to build? Or do I use the credit and lose the author discount and still have to walk around in that ridiculous turtleneck for the rest of the day?

I couldn't handle it. A long line of impatient shoppers was forming behind me. The bookstore owner glared at me. He shuffled his feet. He was a man of little mercy.

Finally, with contempt fairly dripping from his lips like saliva from Mike Ditka, he said, "This is your chance to disprove the myth of female indecisiveness."

This was not a helpful thought. Now, in addition to completely reevaluating how much I wanted the book and what buying it would say about me and my relationship to the world of ideas, I had the dignity of the entire female race on my back.

After several minutes of reviewing the possibilities—buy the book on credit, pay cash, use Visa, be a dizzy dame, pretend I was having a heart attack, choose some other book (but on what subject? hard or paper? fiction or nonfiction?), pick up a few hand-painted bookmarks while I was in there—with these and a few hundred possibilities racing through my brain, the bookstore owner suddenly threw up his hands and stalked off into that little back room where bookstore owners do whatever it is they do there.

Maybe they eat lunch. Or maybe they cry. Maybe they phone their analysts. Or accountants. There are a lot of possibilities here. We don't have to settle on any one. (Decision is death to the imagination.)

Maybe they work on their novel. Yes, maybe it's set in Africa. Or medieval England. Could be about a guy in California. Owns a bookstore. Makes snap decisions. Regrets them later.

Dolphin Show at the L.A. Dude Ranch

I am about to enter the pool at my nifty hotel in L.A. I am very excited because it is hot as the Sahel and I have been walking around all day dreaming about that cool, cool water.

I am staying at this hotel where rock stars (!) stay, but I figure that none of them will be up at three in the afternoon. Besides, I didn't pick this hotel to network with Rod and the Bimbos. I picked it because I heard it has a great pool, and I expected to have it all to myself. It'll be like an Esther Williams wet dream. I'll be able to swim laps in luxury.

Only, when I get there I discover that the pool is packed. Well, not the actual pool. The actual pool is totally empty. But almost every possible poolside chaise is occupied by a totally beautiful person between the ages of eighteen and thirty. No one weighs over 120.

The dudes are wearing little more than what used to be called a G-string (which barely covers the P-spot). The dudettes are wearing suits cut up the side so that virtually their entire B-hinds show.

The gathered are very tan and very dry. The only water touching them is the ice melting in their frozen daiquiris.

And into this scene, half naked, go I?

To jump into the pool would be like being the floor

show. Who cares if they got suctioned or what? In this setting, those of us who are normal and jump into the pool come off like the dolphin show at Marine World.

I have a decision to make. Either: I swallow my pride and go for it, sending a small tsunami to cover the hordes of full-frontal dudity; or: I pull up a chaise and try to start a conversation on the relationship between decadence and wealth.

I conclude that I will not touch their perfect bodies with my mind.

So I stand there, frozen in time at poolside Hollywood, staring in horror at the Beautiful People and remembering some old joke about the moron making a splash on Broadway. I try to visualize swimming, but I keep imagining somebody looking up in horror and saying, "My God, Rod, did you see that woman? She has *thighs!*"

The last time I hit the water in L.A., I was at the Beverly Hilton, where the rather hideous hotel building surrounds an Olympic-sized pool. Doing fast laps in the next lane was Paul Shaffer, the David Letterman bandleader. When we both stopped to breathe at the edge of the pool, I realized I was staring at him.

"Are you *you?*" I said, like some stupid fan. Then he got out of the water and shook my hand.

I'll tell you two things I learned about Shaff. He's a hell of a nice guy. And he doesn't look so hot in a bathing suit either.

But where was a real person at the Hotel Rock Star when I needed one? Nowhere in sight. Only the dead and the adorable know L.A. in August.

Like a competitive swimmer, I stared at the pool, preparing to make my move. I slipped off my white terry hotel-issue robe. I could almost hear a band blasting "The Stripper." OK, folks—show time!

Surf's up. Back and forth I flapped in the little turquoise oasis, without looking up. Finally, though, I was winded and had to face my public. Would they applaud? Would they throw me a fish? Would some young mogul ask me to look at his *Flipper* remake treatment?

But nobody looked. I should have known. Why would these people want to critique my body when they were so busy exhibiting their own?

I lay there in a dead man's float and imagined my obituary: "Beached Porpoise Found Near Sunset Boulevard."

three

CHANNELING

for DOLLARS

The Little Shop
of Electrodes

Welcome to the twenty-first century. Your hosts: Steve and Linda Kay.

I am lying in my underwear in a tastefully decorated cubicle, interviewing Linda while she turns up the juice on the twenty electrodes strapped to my body. Am I a twitching frog in Dr. Caligari's biology lab? Am I a man sentenced to die? Am I Olivia de Havilland in some forties snake-pit movie? No. I am a woman trying to stay in shape.

The Kays operate a mom-and-pop electric muscle-stimulation parlor called Back in Motion. One man's cheap shock is another woman's chic stimulation.

Steve, a former engineer, explains that they first came to the technology they affectionately call "E-stim" several years ago, when Linda, a former piano tuner, developed low back pain. Because they feel it is the best physical-therapy and athletic-training method available, Steve says, "we wanted to share."

The reason I am lying there getting jolted with volts is because I mentioned E-stim in a recent column on "in" trends. Although I normally refuse all nonfood offers, I said OK when Steve called and offered me free treatments.

Imagine my husband's face when he came home from work and I said: "Guess where we're going next

Wednesday night, honey? We're going to a tastefully decorated cubicle where we will lie on pink sheets in our underwear while a strange woman straps twenty electrodes to each of us and zaps the major muscle groups. All expenses paid!"

Did he look thrilled or what? Was he thanking his lucky stars that he was married to a newspaper columnist?

But he came along for the jolt.

In his phone call, Steve had mentioned that E-stim was particularly good for back pain and shoulder and neck tension.

"Was there something in my column that read like it was written by a woman with a pain in the neck?" I asked.

No, Steve said, but most people suffer from this. My husband is one of them, although I occasionally think that he married into it.

I didn't need it for pain, so I decided to try the treatment I have heard described as "passive exercise." Linda explains—as I lie there twitching like a patient unetherized upon a table—that using E-stim is particularly popular in Los Angeles for muscle toning. She says that Boston, San Francisco and Los Angeles are the hotbeds of E-stim. "In Los Angeles, it's used for vanity, while in San Francisco people tend to use it for therapy."

One man's cure is another woman's lure.

The way it works is that the electrodes gently zap the muscle, causing it to contract. So while Linda and I chatted, I watched my quads quiver and my belly bounce, and felt invisible juicers goose my glutes.

Linda claimed I was getting the equivalent of a thousand sit-ups—*sans* perspiration. It wasn't quite like the sweet pain of jogging or the strain of working out with Nautilus machines. It was like doing isometrics without telling yourself to start. You stim, me contract.

Linda explains that in addition to neck and back pain, E-stim is good for people who can't exercise after surgery or who want to speed healing after liposuction. She says the Russians use it to train athletes, although she points out that it has no effect on the cardiovascular system. Much of the research on electro-muscle stimulation was done by NASA scientists attempting to find a way to keep astronauts in shape.

So what's your fantasy? You say you want to pig out for a few years, then go get suctioned and stimulated? You want to watch TV and drink Tang and be a zero-gravity couch potato? You want to smoke and drink and have a heart attack but still look buffed up with those electrically toned muscles? You want to train inefficiently, overexercise sporadically and then come to this New Age Lourdes for the cure?

Forget it. The late-twentieth-century American dream of gain without pain still eludes us.

I read through the literature Steve showed me, articles ranging from "Passive Exercise: Never Lift a Thigh" to "Effects of Short-Term Electrical Stimulation on the Ultrastructure of Rat Skeletal Muscles." These suggest that E-stim may supplement but cannot replace conventional training methods. You can't stim a silk thigh out of a sow's ham bone.

After our "workout"—that's what Steve and Linda call forty-five minutes of dangling from electrodes—my husband's neck felt a little bit better. I felt what Linda described as "nice soreness—like soreness without soreness."

I thanked Steve and Linda for sharing.

We threw our electrodes on the floor and put on our clothes. My husband picked up his Japanese economics book, and I put away my *New Yorker*. We closed the cubicle doors and went for a walk in the old-fashioned rain.

Go to the Head of the Middle Class

Enlightenment is just around the corner. That's where I picked up my new catalog for the Learning Appendix, a nationwide educational program whose only requirements are Visa, M/C or Amex. This might be the year I graduate. I'm only three units short of being a Complete Person.

Here at old Appendix U, our motto is: You don't need a brain, you just need an appendix. Remember—it's easy! It's fun! It's cheap! You'll meet new people! You'll meet cheap new people! And you don't have to learn a darn thing!

This semester I'm taking a full load, even though I'm not playing with a full deck. The hard part is choosing from all the great classes. I usually take three for my left brain, three for my right brain and one more for the road. Here are the descriptions of the classes I'm considering:

• "How to Fake Being a Good Listener"—
Amazing . . . Everything you do in business starts with how YOU LOOK. What kind of signals are YOU sending? We will teach YOU to LOOK like you're interested in other people. Body language is everything. A finger on your eye can cost YOU a contract. A finger in the air can cost YOU an

eye. Learn where to put your finger to get RE-SULTS.

• "Find Perfect Love in 30 Minutes"—Take stock of yourself and then go public. Learn how to flirt, how to manipulate, how to screen for diseases, how to make people love you too much. Perhaps you've seen us on Johnny Carson or read about us in *Newsweek*. We can teach you to make yourself irresistibly attractive. Then we will teach you how to dump everybody who isn't rich enough.

• "Real Estate Investing in About-to-Be-Yupped-Up Neighborhoods"—Everyone has a hobby. Yours may be walking around marginal neighborhoods, thinking: How could I put up a few awnings and drive the blue-collar folks out? If so, WHY NOT MAKE MONEY RUINING THESE PEOPLE'S LIVES? It's easy! Learn how to cut through red tape. Find out how to speed up fore-closures. You can become an instant millionaire in distressed properties. See a rat, smell a buck. Turn slums into sums.

• "A Perfect Armpit in Time for Summer"—Learn the secrets of the stars as you exercise your way to perfect pits in just ten minutes a day. We design a total armpit-fitness plan based on your individual needs. Our physical-fitness instructor and health specialist, Bunny Lumox, is waiting to take your order. You may have seen Bunny's workout featured in *The Economist*. Don't be afraid to play volleyball on the beach. Call today. Pits up!

• "Staying with One Person Even Though You Hate His or Her Guts"—Sometimes life is a sacrifice. Sometimes we have to give up our dreams because we're too overweight to find anybody better. Learn to live with a horrible situation. Let's face it, anyone can leave and try to do better. It takes courage to face the same poor choice day after day after day. Using alcohol, cigarettes and other drugs, you can learn to cope. As seen on Oprah Winfrey.

• "Assertiveness Training for Your Doberman" —A socialized Dobie is like Barbara Walters on Valium. If your pooch is making nice-nice, leave him with us for just two days. We will clip his ears, his tail and your pocketbook. We will lock him in a room with the *Rambo* trilogy playing round the clock. After that, he'll turn *anything* into Kibbles and Bits.

I don't know. So many courses, so little time. I could take something Mickey Mouse like "Making Sushi and Living with Ptomaine" or "Massage for Perverts" or "How to Start Your Own Direct-Mail Brain Surgery Business" . . . But I've heard that if they catch you matriculating, you could get kicked out of school.

Valley of the Silicone Dolls

The flyer said, "Cosmetic Surgery: What It Can and Cannot Do for You!" I already knew. It couldn't make me Einstein, but it might make me look a whole lot more like Phyllis Diller.

I went anyway. As dozens of muscle-bound young people in Lycra-Spandex perfection pumped and groaned in the health club, Dr. Howard Lee, board-certified plastic and reconstructive surgeon, picked up a hand mike and began to wail.

Dr. Lee, a balding man in a gray business suit, seemed nonchalant about the small turnout—a man studying speech and persuasion at Cal State, a pretty woman with a few wrinkles, a handsome man with a gaunt Appalachian face, two sweat-covered, muscle-bound hunks and me.

A huge ceiling fan whirled behind Dr. Lee in the mirror-walled studio. When he turned down the *Flashdance* music and the lights for his surgical slide presentation, a few more aerobicizers slithered in to catch the before-and-after freak show.

Also in the room was a beautiful TV announcer with absolutely no need of plastic surgery. She has started a public relations firm, and Dr. Lee is her first client.

The show began with a slide of an armless Aphrodite, whom Dr. Lee described as "a perfect Ten of 500 B.C."

He switched to a statue he referred to as "an ice-age Venus"—a big, fat mama with gargantuan bosoms. Dr. Lee explained that in the days of starvation, only those with fat genes survived. And that's why we, her descendants, are saddled with saddlebags, love handles and spare tires.

Then we got into what Dr. Lee could do to alter the ill effects of evolution. We saw a slide of a nude woman from the rear with a musical instrument superimposed over her lumpy hourglass figure. Dr. Lee called it "the violin deformity," and he showed us how he could turn her into an electric guitar through the miracle of liposuction, the technique that had revolutionized plastic surgery. Lee said that liposuction (colloquially, "sucking fat") permanently removes fat cells.

We saw more before-and-after pictures of women with the fat sucked out of their chins, women with the fat sucked out of their necks, women with silicone stuck in their chins, women with their breasts "reduced" and women with their breasts "enhanced" by the insertion of silicone globs.

More aerobicizers threw in their towels and came to see the show. Several pec builders left the torture of the Nautilus machines to catch the circus of Dr. Lee. Young men sat on the floor leering at the medicine show.

We saw both the before and after shots of nude women with their eyes blacked out and their pubic hair covered with gauze. I couldn't tell which looked worse —before or after. There were slides of abdomens covered with lines like tribal body paintings in the Mato Grosso—lines to illustrate where the fat-sucking "cannula" was to be inserted.

When Dr. Lee showed a slide of a gelatinous silicone breast insert, one person burst out laughing. When he described a breast reduction and how he moved the nipple and areola upward, one woman screamed out, "Ugggh!" When he showed the "tummy tuck" and explained how he finished it off with a "belly button transplant," several of us instinctively grabbed our abdomens and groaned.

Dr. Lee did not skirt over the difficulties. "Saddlebag surgery is the most common," he said. "That takes two weeks until you can go back to work at a desk job. But you still can't do much walking. An abdomen takes longer."

He emphasized that there are no miracles. A face lift, which costs around three thousand dollars ("eyes cost another two thousand") and lasts anywhere from five to ten years, does not heal overnight. "You see an actress six months after surgery and she looks great," said Dr. Lee, " . . . but right after an eye lift, you look awful. You're swollen, you're black and blue, you look like you've been run over by a truck."

Dr. Lee said he came to the Nautilus center because he is interested in "educating the community." Like most plastic surgeons, he is angry at other doctors cashing in on the cosmetic-surgery bonanza. He assured me that he has all the business he can handle, although you wonder then why he's hooked up with a publicist.

At fifty-four, Dr. Lee himself looks great. I asked him the secret of his perfect skin. "I'm Asian." He smiled. (I can hear Jimmy the Greek now: "Your Asian man was bred with your pretty-skinned woman . . .")

I left the lecture, and on the car radio going home I heard, "Mr. Sandman, bring me a dream, make him the cutest that I've ever seen. . . . Give him a lonely heart like Pagliacci and lots of wavy hair like Liberace. . . ."

I found myself thinking: "Dr. Lee, make me a dream, gimme a pair of buns like you've never seen. Gimme plastic breasts like Carol Doda, and get rid of all the wrinkles that make me look like Yoda. . . ."

And while you're in there, Doc, if you see any brain cells, just suck 'em out.

Help for the Chronically Stressless

The increasing pressure to relax, to avoid stress, to do something fun, is claiming new victims. Tragically, many laid-back people find themselves compulsively relaxing. They are known as lazoholics. And now they have their own support group.

Lazoholics Anonymous, which began in Santa Cruz, has branches in fifty cities, including seven in the Hawaiian Islands. The organization's founder describes himself this way: "Hi. My name is Dustin Offenbach. I'm forty-three years old, and I'm lazy.

"I've only had two jobs in my life," Offenbach continues. "One was as a snow mover in Las Vegas and the other was as a male heterosexual waiter in San Francisco. Both were seasonal. I would practice stress reduction and biofeedback to get through the workday."

He started the organization to help others deal with the guilt that comes from a life spent counting the holes in acoustic ceiling tile. He quickly discovered there were others like him. Different in many ways but sharing the intense drive to do nothing.

Myrna Stemware, thirty-six, a housewife in Akron, Ohio, heard about the organization on "Oprah" and started the first midwestern branch. Stemware traces her problem back to high school, where the yearbook describes her this way: hall monitor, French Club sgt.-at-arms, Slow Dancing Queen runner-up.

She says the plight of lazoholism is particularly acute in the nation's heartland. "Here I was surrounded by fanatic Judeo-Christians rushing off to work," she said, "but come nine a.m., I simply had to have a nap to restore my inner balance before I could tackle the low-maintenance yard."

Lou, twenty-nine, an environmental-quality worker in Ho-Ho-Kus, New Jersey, who does not want his identity revealed, says he used to spend his time compulsively goofing off. "I would be driving to work," he says, "and halfway out the driveway I'd start meditating like crazy."

Lou decided to seek help when his wife of seven years —Mrs. Lou Levitt, 3950 Springsteen Way—left him and he couldn't have cared less.

The problem of lazoholism is on the rise in the downwardly mobile, low-achieving, slow-track communities of California where hundreds of young adults supported by inherited wealth live lives of quiet vegetation.

Existing only on fries and nachos, they swim, surf and defy the ozone layer. The more intellectual among them sit at cafes and write haiku. As one wrote recently, "Sun in my eyes/my shades in the car."

Now these like-minded dim bulbs can come together at LA (Lazoholics Anonymous) meetings. Free espresso is served in an attempt to speed up the discussion, although many participants still cling fanatically to their herbal tea.

If you think you may suffer from lazoholism, take the following test—if you can get it together:

1. Do you find yourself thinking about taking a vacation while still on one?
2. Do you find your sick leave is used up when you actually get sick?

3. Do you find it hard to do even one thing at a time?

4. Do you get annoyed when people talk about work-related matters at the office?

5. When the boss leaves, do you get out your tape deck and yell, "Party!"

6. Do you ever wish there were more Japanese at your company so you wouldn't have to do as much?

If you answered yes to any two of these questions, contact your local LA branch. With a little effort, you can call yourself a Recovering Lazoholic.

Through the Looking Class, Darkly

When a certain newspaper decided to name its Sunday magazine *Image*, a friend of mine remarked, "They were going to name it *Substance*, but they thought that sounded out of date."

Image is what we're all about, so, in these troubled times . . . enter the image consultant, paid tastemaker of the sartorially insecure.

Difficult as it may be for many to comprehend, there appear to be large numbers of people willing to pay someone to tell them, "Definitely, it's you." An image consultant is a person who does that. She also does closets, colors, personal shopping and anything you need in search of the impossible dream: to "feel good about yourself."

There are, in fact, sixty color consultants listed in my local Yellow Pages. As for customers, they seem to be born every minute. "There's plenty of them out there for all of us," says image maven Paula Wilhelm.

Wilhelm is not just an image consultant: she's a professor of Image Consultology. Fourteen of us took her Learning Annex class called "How to Be an Image Consultant."

We shared horror stories like the one about "the real firecracker" who ruined her career when she overwhelmed her colleagues by wearing a red dress to the board meeting. Another disaster was the woman who blew it in a muted green suit. Listening to these stories, one is struck by the even more frightening thought that they are probably true.

"At the end of this evening," I asked naively, "will we be able to hang out our shingle and go into the business?"

"Oh no," replied an amused Wilhelm. "Can you become a brain surgeon in three hours?"

It turns out that this thirty-five-dollar class is just to get us *thinking* about whether we want to matriculate at Wilhelm's Colorconcepts Image Institute. CII offers a "professional" training program that includes core curriculum of Shopping 101, Selecting Eyeglass Frames, Packing for Cruises, Accessorizing and Mental Imaging for Success.

"The image consulting industry" is in transition, says Wilhelm. "Five years ago, everybody was a color consultant." The seminal work was *Color Me Beautiful* by Carol Jackson, whose categorical imperative is that everyone belongs to one of the four seasonal color types.

But Wilhelm rejects the Jacksonian orthodoxy. A woman in the class agreed with her: "I'm supposed to be an autumn, but most of my clothes are winter." No one in the class laughed.

It's not that Paula Wilhelm doesn't like colors. "I can walk into Macy's," she said, "and get excited by the towels."

Those of us not into towels were told to write down the traits we would bring to image consulting.

"I just graduated from high school and thought: 'Gee, now I have to do something,' " said a young woman in snowy white. "So, I thought: 'What do I like to do? I like to shop and sun.' And then I heard about this and thought: 'OhmyGod! I can get paid to go shopping.' "

"I really like to go through people's closets," I said when it was my turn. "But what I really love is drawers. I look in drawers every chance I get."

There was an awkward silence. The teacher, a turn-everything-into-a-virtue type, said, "Well, that's honest, isn't it, class?"

Class agreed.

Later, she explained how to *do* a closet. You have to be sensitive but firm. You have to be "there" for people and let them create "a space."

"It's scary to call a complete stranger and trust your closet to them," said Wilhelm. "That's like showing them your underwear."

Again there were horror stories. Wilhelm once found three pairs of *platform boots* in one woman's closet!

As the evening went on, as we struggled with technical issues like "to preshop or not to preshop," as we listened to industry trends like "nail care is nuts," many were making career decisions on the spot.

Once you are a seasoned professional, you can charge rates like Wilhelm's. These range from $170 for the home visit (which includes closet clearing and reaccessorizing) to $125 for two hours of accompanied shopping.

The value people place on the image consultant (compare her hourly rates to those of a schoolteacher, for example) hints at the neediness of a whole generation. Somewhere along the way, we didn't learn to tie our own shoes. This "industry" nurtures a horde of pinstriped, pulled-together babies who basically just want their mommies.

How the image consultant finds the babies is her problem. Wilhelm does not guarantee that the customers will be there at graduation from Old Image U. All she's offering is a shingle and an application form for the phone book.

My Life as a Piece of Data

Everybody's watching me. You know all those articles about "Will They Spend?" Well, I'm one of *them*.

Just as people are sick of polls in the weeks before elections, and predictions about who will be in the Super Bowl before the play-offs begin, I am sick of the blow-by-blow reports on retail sales figures during the so-called Holiday Season. Suddenly you have to feel as if you are letting your country down if you're not spending. One Jingle Bear too few and you're the consumer equivalent of a Pledge of Allegiance refusenik.

Every year, I go through the same ritual. Sometime before Thanksgiving, I go to the department stores, and, observing with disgust that the decorations are already up, I vow I will not return until New Year's. Then I wait and hope for a miracle. Lo, a garage sale in the East, perhaps. Some alternative to waiting in a long line to lay down twenty-four dollars for a complete set of Teenage Mutant Ninja Turtles.

I dream of a church bazaar where little old ladies sell low-cost, home-canned huckleberry jam in jars hand-painted with antique Victorian motifs. Or, wonder of wonders, maybe I'll get a few days of free time and make something—you know, throw a few pots, crochet a dozen afghans, create a Frank Lloyd Wright Fallingwater house out of gingerbread, turn my old sandals into earrings.

Then around early December, I realize that it just isn't coming together. So I venture forth to some quaint and charming row of small shops with little potted trees out in front decorated with festive, tiny white lights.

Just yesterday, I hit the first of these yuppie anti-mall mini-malls. Ten unique boutiques, all in pure white with solid oak trim and skylights shining on the many useless and incredibly expensive items within. I went into the Mexican Folk Art Shop, a cross between Tijuana and Bloomingdale's. Guess whose prices?

While I thought the pink, polka-dotted, papier-mâché giraffe would be the perfect Hanukkah present for Aunt Myrna, I just couldn't see spending three hundred dollars for something that won't go with the Lladro figurines.

I skipped the lamp shop because it was called the Lighting Studio. Somehow, the lamp-as-art seemed like a dim idea. If God didn't want lamps to be big and ugly, He would have intervened in the late forties.

Then I went to something called the Garden Shop, although nothing was growing there except my incredulity. This was really the ultimate in the new cocooning craze. Everything was so homey that I almost curled up in the six-hundred-dollar chair made of bent willow twigs and went to sleep on the spot.

Here three women were clucking over a hideous black bucket with a flower floating in it. "Isn't it gorgeous?" said one. "It's only ninety-five dollars," said another. I thought we had the makings of a modern fairy tale here: "The Emperor's New Chamber Pot."

The only cheap item in the shop was the three-dollar bar of "Vegetarian Baby Soap." And after all—what decent parenting person would want baby washing his hands with meat?

In my parents' time, it was all so simple. The choices

were few. The expectations were low. Every December they would go to "the wholesale joint" and buy a case of whiskey, a carton of perfume and a few dozen wallets. Then they would divide the known universe into perfume ladies, whiskey men and wallet kids.

No such luck for an eighties lady. Sometime around mid-December, I will wake up and panic.

"I haven't bought anything!" Then I will pick up the paper and read that Dr. Louis Schtunk, Professor of Suckerology at the John Bresford Tipton Graduate School of Marketing, says, "If you can find a parking place at a mall next week, we are in for the worst recession since the thirties."

Like a Stepford shopper, I will find myself dreamlike on the freeway, heading toward the Mall of No Return. I will cruise the parking lot and see a parking place. Uh-oh.

But the fall of America will not be on my conscience. As long as there is breath in my lungs and air in my head, I will go forth. I'll get out my credit card and fall on my knees and say, "Take me, Mr. Retailer. Do with me what you will."

Channeling for Dollars

I was looking for some astral action at the channeling meeting, where the karmically trendy get in touch with their selves.

Channeling, in which you dial inner space and meet any number of kindred spirits, is the rage among bored-again New Agers. This meeting was billed as a Michael Channeling. If you don't like Michael, you can switch to a different channel and find Lester . . . or Laverne . . . or Shirley.

Michael is an entity who has had 1,050 beings over time. Or was he a being who has had 1,050 entities? Either way, the last one was named Michael. Michael speaks through people who have learned to channel him. Apparently a lot of people can do this. Michael is a friendly ghost. And a lucrative one.

Tonight, we are not only-in-Marin or in Berkeley or Santa Cruz. We are at a Masonic Temple in Orinda, California. Orinda—just seven BART stops from heaven! Who would have guessed that after all those millennia, Michael would end up in the suburbs?

Eighty of us have shelled out the $15 admission fee. That's a cool $1,200. More than a buck for each manifestation of Michael.

You can even buy a poster of Michael for $25. It appears to be three stripes made up of lots of tiny people. That's how Michael manifested himself to the artist.

You can buy the *Michael Digest* for $14 and learn how Michael study groups have applied Michael to such issues as "Humphrey the Whale and AIDS." That's Applied Michael, as opposed to Theoretical Michael.

You can buy rocks that put you in touch with fun energy or male energy or balance energy just by holding them. You can buy Psychoactive Essence Imprints. The flier explains: "Essence Imprints are works of art in which a spiritually aware artist had channeled the powerful vibrations of a person's essence directly into color and form."

Could I make this up?

Michael is brought to us tonight through channels J. P. Van Hulle and Aaron Christeaan. J.P., a large woman in a bright green silk blouse and matching eye makeup, is married to Aaron. Aaron is a muscular blond who wears magenta stretch pants, white suede boots and a flowing, sleeveless, jeweled blouse that shows his tan and chest hair to advantage. Aaron has the aura—and I use the word loosely—of a beachboy.

J.P. and Aaron sit on large red velvet thrones on the stage of the Masonic Temple. Behind them is an American flag and the Freemasons' symbol. The couple is flanked by two women. "These are our channeling buddies Nicole and Lillian," J.P. explains. "What comes out of any of our mouths will be from Michael."

Out of the mouths of these babes came Michael. And, yes, she did say "buddies." Soul buddies is what Michaelists call their alter essences.

Seated in the concrete-block, fluorescent-lit room are the eighty dressed-and-coiffed-for-success men and women, average age thirty-four. The New Age is getting older but shows no signs of wising up.

Most take notes and listen attentively. The feel of the room is somewhere between a college classroom, a Unitarian service, a real estate investment seminar and a singles group meeting.

Michael-via-J.P. spends about forty minutes giving us a report on April, the month "you look at who you're intimate with in your life—not just lovers but children, parents, pets, fish and plants." Aaron sits there looking cute and scratching his forehead. Or is he rubbing his third eye?

Basically, April is going to be one ca-razy month. "Near Easter a lot of people hook into that Christ energy," warns J.P./Mike. "But the partying type of energy will come up by the end of the month." (If Spuds McKenzie sees his shadow.)

There is absolutely not a trace of mysticism in the joint. Mystery I can relate to. Magic I can dig. But a ghost who isn't spooky is just . . . boring.

J.P. and Aaron don't seem all that different from Jim and Tammy. But the godless yuppie prefers Michael to those redneck revivalists.

A nursing mother in the audience said, "We went to our tax guy yesterday and found out we owe a lot of money, but I didn't care. I felt happy. Now, I'm kind of wondering: Maybe we don't really owe it."

"That's how it feels when you don't have any karma about money," explains J.P./Mike.

Since there was no trance, no chanting, no deep breathing to get in touch—none of the stuff associated with the more glamorous ghosts made famous by Shirley (Limb) MacLaine—one could not verify the authenticity of the Michael connection.

A woman asked, "I've never been here before, and I'm trying to find out what your process is. Are you giving us information you got earlier today or right now?"

"Right now," the channels all agreed. Yet the room seemed spiritually sterile, filled with astral holes.

During the break, I meet a gourmet-foods clerk, a teddy-bear manufacturer, an advertising executive and a personal fitness trainer. Some have been coming for three years for a little piece of Michael and a sense of belonging.

Belonging is what's going on here. People pass their business cards, they network, they hug. The Michael meeting is like a coed Masonic lodge.

People show each other snapshots of their "ETs"— their Essence Twins.

Could I make this up?

A young man tells his girlfriend, "I want you to meet Aaron and J.P." She says, "This is like meeting the in-laws."

A man comes up to me and hugs me. "Hi, I'm Larry. I have no essence on the messianic plane." For once, I can't say: "I've heard that line before, pal."

Larry explains that he channels Michael but he also channels other entities. "Who's that?" I ask. "Oh—whoever," he replies.

"What do you do for a living, Larry?" I ask. "I'm a general contractor," he says, handing me his card.

"Michael has no essence down there," Larry comments, pointing between his legs.

"Down there?" I ask discreetly.

"Yes, down there," he says, "in the first chakra."

I move on toward Aaron, who is showing his malachite pendant to another man. Aaron explains that the pendant is really good for male energy. The man asks, "Will this help me be less intellectual?"

We returned for more questions. The evening evolves into a cosmic dating game as the lonely, the horny and the unfulfilled get Michael's advice to the lovelorn. Many women ask quiet little questions about their relationship problems. I'm tempted to yell, "LOUDER!" but why wake the dead?

An attractive blonde in a stunning beige silk dress asks, "Since I have to stay home and not work this month, is there any sort of mate mischief I can get into?" J.P. bellows at the room, "This woman is available."

For three hours, I keep a jargon count. Energy gets mentioned 35 times; essence 32; karma 27; chakra 7; healing 4. Astral essence and karmic bonding, a single mention each.

I scan the announcements for further Michael opportunities. There's the Michael Fundraiser, where you can win an hour-long channeling with Aaron Christeaan, "value" $100. There is also the *professional* program in Acu-Kinetic Repatterning ("Spinning"). For $520 you can become a *certified* practitioner. There is a program to "Change Your Life Through Colors" (regularly $275, introductory special $150 with coupon below).

And finally there is the third annual Michael Retreat at Harbin Hot Springs. Aaron and J.P. will channel Michael, and Mark Thomas will channel Seth and Deva. The $125 fee covers "shamanic rituals, dream-sharing, breakfast and dinner."

The questions continue relentlessly. In the dark suburban night of the soul, Michael has the answers.

At 10:00 P.M., I looked at the clock in horror. For this, I'm missing "L.A. Law"?

Guess Who's Coming to Passover Dinner

There is no word for what I am. Even Yiddish, a language that has immortalized shlemiels, shmendriks and zhlubs, has no name for me. I am a seder hustler.

Every year around Passover, I start hanging around my Jewish friends, hoping someone will pop the question and invite me to the holiday meal.

"Man, I sure could go for some unleavened bread. You folks havin' a big seder this year?" I'll say, and then I'll shoot them the lost-at-Ellis-Island look.

"Seder hustler!" they scream and head for the kosher hills.

I know what you're thinking. Why not make your own seder?

The thing is, it's a lot easier to *be* Jewish than to *do* Jewish. Although I realize that for thousands of years others have managed to get it together, I'm afraid to organize a seder where book worship and food worship combine with real worship. There's so much room for error. For being B-A-D.

The Jewish Community Center, which offers classes in everything from "Assertiveness for Women" to "Healing Crystals and Yeast," has no "Seder from Scratch" class. And where the heck is modern tech? I keep hoping someone will produce *Seder!—The Video*. Or maybe *Jane Fonda's Passover Workout* ("Burn that brisket! Whew!").

My mother never taught me. Every year I'd watch in awe as she slaved over caldrons of soup. Even after my bachelor uncles got married and moved out of the house, my mother would still send them chicken soup by taxi on Passover.

I'd see her sculpt gefilte fish with her bare hands. I'd watch her hide the weekday dishes and the Sabbath dishes and get out the special Passover dishes. But she wanted me to be a modern American woman. I suppose she hoped I would marry a rich man and we could order out from Dial-a-Seder.

"Go watch TV," she'd say if she caught me watching her. And most of the Old World customs died with her.

When I was in my teens, my family went completely modern. We bought a long-playing album called *A Passover Seder with Jan Peerce*. Instead of my father reading the prayers and leading the songs, we'd sing along with Jan. I always hoped the record would get scratched at one of the wine prayers and everyone would get that Manischewitz buzz before realizing the needle was stuck.

During the sixties, in Berkeley, I got invited to my first New Age all-vegetarian seder. Instead of the traditional plate of bitter herbs, there were all sorts of weird hippie herbs. Instead of the traditional question, "Why is this night different from all other nights?" someone asked, "Like, what's happening tonight that isn't happening, like, every night?"

I hustled my way into several other weird seders during that era, including a Judeo-Communist one in which the traditional Passover prayer book, the Haggadah, sat alongside Mao's Little Red Book. The journey of a thousand matzos begins with the first bite.

Finally, in the eighties, I met Tom and Sharona. As far as I'm concerned, this was the jackpot. Smart, witty and attractive, they did a traditional seder with great food and high-quality wine. They always had interesting guests like Israeli scientists and French environmentalists. I thought I was in Fat Seder City.

Then they had two babies. This limited Sharona's seder outreach and left me having to hustle my way into another seder.

Two years ago, a long-lost cousin called and invited our family. It was a nice gathering, but so many people had married gentiles or left the fold that no one knew how to do a seder.

This year, I didn't kibitz around the bush. When a friend said she was having a seder, I asked her at point-blank range to invite me. I told her I'd beat her up if she didn't—which, where I come from, means I'd make her feel very guilty.

I even offered to roll up my sleeves and roll the matzo balls. Years ago, some mysterious force compelled me to make the healing chicken broth of my ancestors, and it came out just right. The Passover rituals have to be learned from a book, and the prayers have to be translated. But the soup is in my DNA.

Alice in Esalen-Land

I must be the last psycho-virgin in California. I've never been ested, encountered or even rolfed. Call me hard-core unevolved. Now, on the occasion of its twenty-fifth anniversary, I make my maiden voyage to the Esalen Institute, trying to understand why people keep saying the place is magic. Once-shocking ideas that germinated there have spread to every YMCA and university extension in America. Is there anything left for Esalen at mid-life?

You don't come upon this collection of ideas, buildings and incomparable acreage at Big Sur because you're in the neighborhood. You travel to the Esalen Institute, roughly halfway between Los Angeles and San Francisco, on a pilgrimage—stalking the wild experience.

"Do I have to eat the food?" my husband asked as he prepared to perform his Ricky Ricardo function. The man is even more of a purist than I. Never therapized, never meditated, never vegetarianized, he agreed to join me at the weekend seminar entitled, "Leonard Energy Training and the Samurai Game." We dared Esalen to show us a good time.

As described in the Esalen catalogue, in addition to the energy-training exercises of instructor George Leonard, the seminar would give us the opportunity to "enter the state of consciousness of a medieval samurai, to live intensely in the moment, and to experience symbolic death and rebirth." Finally, before returning to the office on Monday, we would join in "a symbolic battle to the death through which participants will have a chance to experience the ultimate futility of war and the value of every moment of existence."

Are they serious?

So it was with a feeling of the ultimate ridiculousness of every moment of existence and some small hope of catching samurai night fever that we set out on Highway 1. But not in total innocence. We had heard the story of Esalen from friends who had been there, from writers who'd mythologized and satirized it and from several decades of living in this strange state of California.

Ideas dismissed as crackpot in crackpot New England or as occult in the born-again heartland have been explored at Esalen by some of the best-publicized minds of our century. Not only Joan Baez and Simon and Garfunkel and some of the Beatles, but every celebrity intellectual of the past twenty-five years has been there. The Carl Saganicity is astounding. Participants have ranged from Henry Miller to Aldous Huxley to Paul Tillich to Arnold Toynbee to Susan Sontag to Herman Kahn to Buckminster Fuller to B. F. Skinner to Linus Pauling to Jerry Brown to Fritjof Capra. We're talking weight. It's as if someone with land, money, free time and relentless curiosity (an apt description of Esalen's leadership) decided to hold a party and everyone came.

"The place is magic," my next-door neighbor, a handsome young psychotherapist, had told me. I realized as he spoke that in describing their Esalen experiences, people tend to tell you more about themselves than they do about Esalen. My neighbor had to *share* that he has an "open marriage" and "a need to be naughty" to explain why he went to Esalen with his "lover." (I listened intently the whole time for some hint of whether the lover was a boy or a girl.) He said they both threw off their clothes and began to make love in front of Fritz Perls's house, where behavioral scientist Gregory Bateson was about to lead a seminar. They managed to be naughty enough to force the tolerant Esalen staff to insist that they stop and get dressed or leave.

Another friend described the plain concrete tubs where bathers enjoy the hot natural mineral springs as looking "like something in Nazi Germany." Later, I realized that my friend's description was less an accurate picture of the scene than a revelation of her psyche.

Stories like these increased my curiosity and anticipation, but nothing seemed more mythological than the history of the institute. While reading about Esalen, talking to people who have been there and interviewing key players, I noted that a series of tales—almost folkloric tales—keep cropping up. Yet everyone swears they're true.

Let's start with the legendary baths. More than anything else, the baths at Esalen have contributed to its reputation as a kind of primal hot-tub scene. Certainly there is nothing rarer than a natural hot spring on a cliff above the Pacific Ocean. Now that's what I call magic.

Shortly after my arrival, I hit the baths. It was half to get it over with, half "heal me, oh wondrous waters." I found the communal baths with the communal changing room more nurturing than sensuous, certainly less threatening than the pool at the Beverly Hilton. At an L.A. pool one is always comparing oneself to the bulimic, aerobiholic perfection of the other women in bikinis. Here you are a part of a work of art: not airbrushed *Playboy* images, but the natural curves and acceptable flesh of real people.

You can find plenty of fuel for California satire in the baths. Spacey twenty-year-olds chat endlessly about their dreams or about Jerry and Bob (of the Grateful Dead). Psychobabbling thirty-year-olds harp on their relationships (". . . so I told him it was a continuous process. . . . My second husband let me be me"). Lonely women confront frustrated business executives ("Look, you're married, you're here and your wife's home with the kids. Would you want to marry someone like you?").

But others in the baths fit no pattern. The investment banker from Brazil who keeps jumping out of the tub to place flowers on a statue of Buddha. The old man from Boston who never stops reading his suspense novel. The upholsterer from Costa Mesa whose first girlfriend brought him to Esalen when he got out of the Air Force. The recreation director from the Philadelphia mental hospital who's just taking a vacation.

Odd strangers meet here, like the Jewish recovering alcoholic stockbroker from Alaska who explains to the German work-study student that she is acting *meshugge*. "Germans can't understand Yiddish," he says, "*Meshugge* means crazy."

At one point, the oncologist's wife from Pasadena looks up dreamily and says, "Can you imagine what Marriott would do with this place?"

Good question, because perhaps the most remarkable thing about Esalen is how it has resisted commercialization. Despite all the forces that would gladly have turned the place into a drug haven in the sixties or a cult scene in the seventies or a yuppie Disneyland in the eighties, it remains shockingly plain and pleasant—undominated by anything other than the feeling that *anything* is possible.

Michael Murphy, Esalen's founder and guiding

spirit, recalls that over the years he and co-founder Dick Price often said, "Let's blow the baths off the side of the cliffs."

That's because Murphy feels that the media pay undue attention to nudity at the baths, ignoring Esalen's cerebral side, just as Western thinkers have focused on the mind apart from the body. It is clear that Murphy sees Esalen as an intellectual institution (but without the rigidity of a university or the overzealousness of an ashram), where the possibilities of what people are capable of—the human potential—may be explored. Esalen seems an attempt to merge elements of Murphy's own education—Stanford University, the ashram of Sri Aurobindo in India and marathon running. It's a haven for people who never wanted to major in anything.

Although Murphy insists that "the baths were simply there," the history of the institute, this noble undertaking, this marriage of mind and body, really begins at the baths.

Murphy, who was born in Salinas in 1930, inherited the land through a trust from his grandmother. His grandfather, Dr. Henry Murphy, the man who delivered John Steinbeck and who was the model for a character in *East of Eden*, bought the three-hundred-acre property in 1910 because of the hot spring. The Esalen Indians had long ago discovered its charm. Dr. Murphy planned to establish a European-style healing spa on the California coast.

After grandson Michael and Stanford classmate Dick Price decided to establish a learning center on the property in 1961, the Taking of the Baths became the first event in the folkloric history of Esalen.

Between the years when Grandpa Murphy had bathtubs hoisted up the cliffs and 1962, when Dick Price and Michael Murphy organized their first series of seminars, entitled "Human Potentialities," several groups used the property. An evangelical group rented the motel-like building and held revivals. Meanwhile, an assortment of beatniks, wild men from the nearby Santa Lucia Mountains and gays from Los Angeles and San Francisco claimed the baths as their own. These groups were not ready to surrender turf to Murphy, despite his property rights and his noble purpose.

In the first of many hard-to-believe tales, Murphy says, he asserted ownership in an event known as the Night of the Dobermans. On this night, a young security guard from Kentucky named Hunter Thompson ("executive caretaker" is the way the Gonzoid One recalls his position) was unable to keep the intruders from the tubs. So Murphy, accompanied by reinforcements that included Joan Baez's boyfriend and several Doberman pinschers, went down to confront the invaders. There was a standoff until a fight broke out between two male Dobermans over a female. Their howls sent the gay men running. A few weeks later, the evangelicals split. Thus, the Esalen Institute was established.

The next event in this magical history tale was the Coming of Maslow. One dark night in the summer of 1962, progressive psychologist Abraham Maslow and his wife, Bertha, were lost in dense fog on the central California coast while on a trip south. Seeing a light that they believed to be a motel, they approached the building. Bertha Maslow thought it looked like the Bates Motel in *Psycho*. They were greeted by Gia-fu Feng, a friend of Murphy and Price, who served as Esalen's chief cook, t'ai chi teacher and abacus-toting accountant. (He was also a graduate of the Wharton School and a veteran of Wall Street.) At first Feng was indifferent to the couple, but when Maslow signed his name, Feng went wild. Suddenly twelve scholars appeared from the Bates Motel clutching copies of Maslow's new book, *Toward a Psychology of Being*, and the long relationship between the father of humanistic psychology and the Esalen Institute was forged.

"It's true! It's true!" Murphy laughs as he describes this strange coincidence. "I took it as a sign from beyond. I saw my beliefs confirmed in these omens."

The next tale in Esalen's history, like many folk tales, has several versions. It is the story of How Fritz Perls Beat Hollywood. In the late sixties, Esalen and the psychologists who flocked there had developed a number of new techniques for producing cathartic experiences, for allowing people to confess and confront their deepest, darkest secrets. One of these techniques—the encounter group—became, like the baths, a plus and minus for Esalen. Overused and overpublicized, it threatened to dominate Esalen's eclectic menu.

When Hollywood discovered encounter therapy, leaders feared that the institute would be overrun with movie stars. This fear ended after actress Jennifer Jones invited genius/madman Fritz Perls, the father of gestalt therapy, to a party at her Bel Air mansion. With Rock Hudson, Tuesday Weld and James Coburn, among others, looking on, Perls had Natalie Wood take the hot seat. He told her, "You're nothing but a little spoiled brat who always wants her way."

Perls then took Wood across his knee and spanked her. Another version of the story has the incident ending with Roddy McDowall threatening to slug Perls. Either way, Hollywood stayed away from Esalen after that, except to immortalize such therapeutic excesses in satirical movies.

"By 1972, we worried about the excesses," says Murphy, and he explains that this includes the importance placed on the notion of climactic insights. "We went too far. I wish we hadn't made mistakes, but we were adventurists." Another notion from the sixties that Murphy eventually discarded was the communal way decisions were made at Esalen. "We learned that excessive communalism doesn't work."

Three years ago, Murphy and Price began to reevaluate Esalen. For a time, Murphy says, he almost gave up and looked into selling the institute. He denies that this period of disillusionment had anything to do with the fact that he was then, at fifty-four, becoming a father for the first time.

"We're finally doing it right," Murphy recalls Price saying one day two years ago. The next day Price was killed in one of those mysterious events that are entwined with Esalen.

Price, like Murphy, came from a rich family and was also bright, handsome and charismatic. After graduate work in psychology at Harvard, he joined the Air Force, where he had an episode that he experienced as a religious phenomenon but which was labeled a psychotic break. His family had him institutionalized, and he was given sixty-seven insulin-shock treatments. This explains his passionate interest in developing alternative forms of psychotherapy at Esalen.

He also became a great outdoorsman at Big Sur, developing trails that led from the institute grounds to the steep mountains above. He was killed on one of these trails by the random fall of a huge boulder.

"There was a one-in-a-billion chance of this boulder hitting him," Murphy says. "We went up there and traced its path. A two-ton boulder exploded ten feet below him. A two-hundred-pound shard flew up and broke his spine. He was killed instantly. The boulder leapt one hundred yards through a narrow opening in the redwoods. It partook of the occult."

All this potential for magic, disastrous and wondrous, was in my mind as I walked around the grounds—passed the waterfall near where Dick Price died, climbed down to the beach where waves erode up to five feet of cliff each year, walked among the eucalyptus trees where hundreds of monarch butterflies breed, ambled by the child-care center where a little boy sat on an open structure labeled "Pottieville."

My husband and I ate heartily that Friday night—a fantastic dinner that included enchiladas, beans, corn *porzole*, a salad bar that would be the envy of any in Beverly Hills and several salsas made with fresh chilies and tomatoes grown on Esalen's own farm. "Those are expensive tomatoes," business manager Steve Donovan later told me, pointing out that it's actually cheaper to buy them than grow their own.

Despite such luxuries, Donovan has managed to turn Esalen's debt of $200,000 in 1977 into a surplus of more than quadruple that this year, all of which will go into seeding such new projects as a Soviet/American exchange program. The $3,624,000 budget includes a few salaries in the $40,000 range. Donovan, forty-six, a Columbia University M.B.A. ("I was a fast-track yuppie in the sixties"), gets $27,000 for a half-time position.

"It's part of the culture of the place not to be a platform for individuals to get wealthy—it's a bit socialistic that way," says Donovan. "In the sixties and seventies, most of the people who worked here were in their twenties and thirties. Now these people have been here fifteen to twenty years and they're married, have kids. We're trying to create an economic environment that supports families."

Donovan figures that George Leonard took home about six hundred dollars for the twelve-hour weekend program I attended. The program began Friday night after dinner when we entered the seminar room and set out on the road to medieval Japan.

There were more than forty "seminarians," four guys to every gal, and our leaders—George Leonard; his wife, Annie Styron Leonard; and Jack Cirie. Leonard was a civil-rights reporter and a *Look* editor when he first came to Esalen in 1965 to interview Mike Murphy for a story called "The Human Potential." He has been involved with the place ever since as vice president and seminar leader and is yet another seemingly ageless, impeccably educated, open-minded explorer. As he told me, "I still can't explain to my mother what I do."

At sixty-four, Leonard is a contributing editor at *Esquire*, the author of such books as *Education and Ecstasy* and *The End of Sex* and the co-owner of an aikido center in Marin County. Like Murphy and others at the helm, he is eager to explain how Esalen differs from what he calls "the schlock" that invariably is associated with the human-potential scene. He will later cringe when a seminarian insists that he saw a "flying saucer over the ocean from the baths" and dismiss Shirley MacLaine–ism as "end-of-the-millennium behavior."

But, Leonard also adds, "there is a spiritual side of life, and the neighborhood Protestant church is the last place to have a mystical experience."

Cirie's is another only-at-Esalen story. After attending Yale, he entered the Marine Corps, where he served for twenty years. He was a lieutenant colonel like his colleague and acquaintance Oliver North. Oliver North is one famous name bandied about who never came to Esalen. Perhaps if he had, we'd be peddling consciousness instead of M-16s to the contras.

In 1983, while Cirie was on leave, he came to Esalen and played the samurai game with George Leonard. For the first time he saw the potential to experience some of the intensity of the military without the backdrop of a war. The next year, he put on his uniform—medals and all—and a fellow officer retired him from the corps on the cliffs at Esalen.

Annie Leonard, one-time executive at the Guggenheim Museum and an editor of the *Whole Earth Catalogue*, is a pleasant, lively woman who avoids psychobabble. (She calls anxiety "the jitters.") She leads us in several exercises in which we find our "center"—a concept nobody questions.

The exercises have, to my husband's relief, a familiar, this-worldly quality. We learn such techniques as an "unmuggable walk" and moving to avoid being clobbered. It's a little aikido, a little self-defense, a little relaxation. People "share" how they feel. Some say they feel grounded and centered. Some say they feel the energy. I feel a little silly, but I don't say so because I'm having a good time. It's more fun than TV and more physical than talking to your friends. It's different. Being an adult, I realize, is the most behaviorally boring thing on earth.

"Esalen is adventure more than therapy," Leonard would tell me later. "We're not here to make the sick well. We take people who are already OK and make them better."

By the time the samurai game began Saturday afternoon, we were feeling fine. It may have been the exercises or it may have been the hour-long massages we took on the outdoor tables near the ocean. The husband was actually approaching blissed-out. "Are you having a good time?" I asked him. "Being massaged by a naked lady is not bad," he said. He would later speak of Katherine, his masseuse, in the same tone I am sure the destitute reserve for Mother Teresa.

The game consisted of dividing the seminarians into

two groups, the armies of the North and the South. Under orders from our leader (our "daimio," chosen randomly by a fellow warrior), we would be called forth to battle—the battles consisting of combatants squaring off to see who could hold such yoga positions as the eagle (legs out, arms spread) or the white crane (arms up, foot up) the longest. We also matched valor playing the children's finger game of paper/rock/scissors.

The war gods (the Leonards and Cirie) would orchestrate the battles, playing Japanese martial music and adjusting the lights. Occasionally, they irrationally ordered the "death, maiming or blinding" of one of the players. If you "died" you had to remain motionless with your eyes shut for the rest of the game. (As in life, the longer you survived, the more you enjoyed it.) You also couldn't smile or laugh. Violating the rules could result in the "blinding or maiming" of your fellow soldiers.

Leonard sees the game as "a realization of some of the earlier goals of Esalen—to give the mind, body and spirit the same value." But, he adds, it is "a more sophisticated and aesthetically pleasing way to do it. It's ungross. The early encounters were kind of gross."

By dinnertime on the night of the samurai game, my husband had been "maimed" because of incompetence on the part of our leader, our daimio. Poor Ricky Ricardo had to eat with one hand tied behind his back, and I had to cut his barbecued ribs. I began to hate our daimio, a petty little martinet. Later, when he was ordered to "blind" a soldier because of another mistake and he chose me for the honor, I began to despise him. Leonard told me that the worst daimio he had seen in the ten years he'd been playing the game was a fellow who insisted that his troops say, "We who are about to die salute you."

The game drove home my own rebellious nature.

During dinner, against our leaders' orders, my husband and I sneaked off and drank a beer as we watched the sunset from Esalen's scented garden. We also laughed. Ha. Ha.

Later, when I was "blinded," I cheated by peeking under the blindfold. I wanted to see who my sympathetic teammates were. Within seconds of my blinding, one fellow warrior grabbed my behind. Others insisted on massaging my back. There's something about a blinded samurai woman that really brings out the touchy-feely in these people.

I felt something like genuine pride as my husband, with one hand behind his back, out-eagled a black belt in karate. I felt sad when he was killed—hit with a "ninja star," symbolically represented in the game by a Minute Maid orange-juice-can lid. Eventually we both felt some secret glee when our daimio was forced to commit seppuku.

It was my unfortunate task to "kill" a member of the other army by out-white-craning him. He was a seventy-year-old Jewish man from New York named Irving who insisted on being called Biff. He said he had come to Esalen looking for his youth. I was very touched by this man. And I killed him.

It was him or me.

At the end of the game, on Sunday morning, we did a little aikido-like dance to the music of "The Skaters' Waltz" with the person we had killed. I glided around with Irving/Biff, sending good vibes his way. He sent forgiveness.

Our final exercise was to close our eyes and place an imaginary crystalline ball in our center. By now, I knew instinctively where my center was, even if I still couldn't tell my chakra from my *pupik*.

After inserting the ball, we were to open our eyes and

walk around Esalen trying to see things without prejudice. When I opened my eyes, I had this strong memory of what kindergarten felt like. I was in a room full of fascinating people all sitting cross-legged on the floor. Instead of seeing a bunch of middle-aged, middle-class jerks, I saw a group of boys and girls I wanted to be my friends. Even the hated daimio was just another interesting kid.

I won't say it was a miracle. I won't say that I experienced what was felt in those cathartic encounters at Esalen twenty years ago or what the evangelicals experienced at Esalen in the fifties or what the Indians experienced at Esalen before White Man first drove his Porsche up the coast. But I felt good.

Yes. OK. I believe. The place is magic.

It's hard to imagine this kind of exploration occurring anywhere but at the West's westernmost edge. Perhaps Esalen could have happened back East, but California's major intellectual advantage may well be its beauty, which forces you to take the physical world seriously.

"There's always been a fear of California back East," says Michael Murphy, and he laughingly quotes Edmund Wilson writing about California in *The New Yorker*. "One has only to look at their ocean to know what kind of people they are."

As he said this, I thought about old Irving-called-Biff, rejuvenated at the sumptuous piece of California real estate that Mike Murphy has used to turn on the world. Biff said that after the samurai game, as he walked around with his imaginary crystalline ball, he was drawn to a girl out on the patio overlooking the ocean. "I just sat there and talked to her. I didn't think about the future. I didn't try to make her. I just enjoyed it. That is what I came here to feel. At my age, it's hard to do."

And with that Biff lay down on the floor of the seminar/exercise room and went to sleep. As he snoozed, the rest of us walked around the room one more time in a final exuberant strut to rhythmic music. Was it the ocean? Was it the massage? Was it the food? Was it some moment of self-discovery in the samurai game? Why did we all feel so good?

One seminarian, a singer from Melrose Avenue (the guy who had seen the flying saucer), offered an answer to the mystery when he began singing "Blame It on the Bossa Nova" to the music.

Until Esalen completes its mission—to explore the mysteries, to combine Eastern circular and Western linear thinking, to discover how the mind and the body and the spirit interact—we won't fully understand why the place is magic. Till then, the Bossa Nova Theory will have to do.

four

The FAMILY That SHABOOMS TOGETHER

A Sibling Reverie

My big sister, Myrna Lou, called from Chicago last night. Nobody calls her Myrna Lou anymore. And nobody but Myrna Lou calls me Alice Joyce. Ever.

For fourteen years, we shared a room, two crazy parents and familial chaos. Then we moved uptown and got separate rooms; she got married, the parents calmed down and then they died. Now, two thousand miles apart, we talk on the phone six times a year. Just like a Pacific Bell commercial. And that's what's left of the family that sculpted my psyche and still haunts my dreams.

"Alice was a weird nocturnal thing," my sister told someone, describing me as a child. I reminded her that my insomnia began when she would wake me up each night at midnight claiming "a man" was trying to climb in the window. Then she'd say to me in a solemn voice, "Go into the kitchen and get the knives, Al."

Seven years old, sweating with terror, I'd come back from the kitchen with a handful of steak knives. Myrna Lou would be snoring by then. I'd lie awake the rest of the night, watching the window, waiting for the man.

I brought up the man at the window again when we had our big fight in '72. My father was gone. My mother was in the hospital. And Myrna Lou and I were screaming at each other in the car coming in from the airport where she'd just picked me up. I was feeling my Berkeley oats. She was trying to raise a family.

"How could you vote for Nixon? You've gone nuts, Myrna!"

"Yeah, well you're the one with the insomnia, Alice."

"Because I had to share a room with a crazy maniac like you," I screamed, ". . . who hallucinated men at the window and is now a goddamn Republican."

"Look, Alice," she shot back, "if you don't like this country, you can leave it."

"Look, pal, I'm the one out there working and contributing to the society. You're the suburban matron with the maid."

That was it. She pulled the Buick Riviera to the side of the road. I got out and hitchhiked to my mother's apartment. We didn't speak again until the funeral, a couple of years later.

I hated her after that fight as much as I had idolized her years before. In 1955, when I was eleven and she was sixteen, I thought she was the coolest kitty-cat on earth.

She worked after school at Mar-Rue's Shoppe selling cashmere sweaters but never brought home a paycheck. All her salary was reinvested in her own cashmere collection. She had fifty of them: thirty pullovers, fifteen cardigans, a boat-neck, a cowl and three argyles.

She had a boyfriend named Norman Baum, a greaser, whom we called "The Bomb." The Bomb called Myrna "Baby" and made her stop calling me "Little Walrus." He helped her buy the first car ever owned by a member of our family. It was a red '53 Ford convertible that Myrna named "Desiree."

Norman did something to the muffler so you could hear Desiree coming a mile away. Myrna dyed her hair flaming red to go with the car.

When my father tried to stop Norman from taking

Myrna out one night, The Bomb threatened to punch my father out. I watched Myrna and her hepcat boyfriend walk out the door while my father stood there fuming. I thought to myself: Cool, daddy-o.

After Myrna broke up with Norman and gave him back his ID bracelet, she had a million boyfriends. Sometimes when they called up, I'd pretend I was older and they'd talk sexy to me. One of them was a record promoter named Don Neff who claimed he actually *knew* Screamin' Jay Hawkins. Even when Don Neff found out I was twelve, he'd still call up and talk sexy to me. I thought that was so kind of him.

Myrna was listening to Eddie Fisher and Joni James but also to some real gone music by Bill Haley and the Comets. She showed me a dance called "the dirty boogie" that you could do to music like that.

By the time she started college, Myrna was driving a white Plymouth Fury with swivel bucket seats. She broke up with an incredibly rich guy whose father owned half the town. He called up, and I had to tell him she refused to speak to him. "That's what I get for crossing the tracks," he said to me.

On Sunday mornings, I'd sit in Myrna's room and she'd read to me from her diary about her date the night before—the orchid corsage, the show at Mister Kelly's or the Blue Note, the fight in the car about "going all the way." She was a drama major and once wrote something I'll never forget. "Some day, some distant day," she penned, "Myrna shall burst forth like a thousand Roman candles."

On Valentine's Day 1960, Myrna got married. I was a bridesmaid. I wore a pink cocktail dress and carried a heart-shaped bouquet of pink tea roses. Each table had a pink, heart-shaped ice-cream cake that said "Myrna and Arthur."

Three years later, she had a house in the suburbs and two babies. She was a square. It took me twenty years and a few kids of my own to forgive her.

So yesterday, she called to tell me that she'd decided not to go to her high school's thirtieth reunion. "I look sensational, but why go back and flaunt it? It would be like returning to the scene of an accident."

An *accident*—the place where she varoomed up in Desiree wearing her mint-green cashmere sweater set and French-kissed The Bomb good-bye? Say it ain't so, Myrn. I worshiped that accident.

Her youngest graduated from college this year. "I shed a tear when he moved out," she said, "and then I put some stuff into his closet."

Myrna started working this year as a publicist for a hand surgeon. She loves her work. Medical publicity is a growing field.

It's not a thousand Roman candles, but Myrna feels successful.

"Write about me, Al," she said last night. "Tell my story."

The Family That Shabooms Together Stays Together

"The sixties music was less rock and more roll," she said. I don't know what it means, but I loved her for saying it.

The speaker is my daughter Emma, just turned fourteen. The scene is somewhere on California Highway 1, a long, winding stretch looking down at a huge expanse of beach. And we'll have fun, fun, fun, as her mommy drives the Camry along.

Suddenly, I get this feeling—it's not quite *déjà vu*. Let's call it "*déjà* something." I haven't had this feeling before. But it's a feeling I have wanted to have, a feeling I have imagined having these past fourteen years. I am having an intellectual discussion about rock 'n' roll with my daughter.

The song on the radio was Steve Miller's remake of "Sittin' in My Ya-Ya, Waitin' for My La-La." (Or is it "Sittin' in My La-La, Waitin' for My Ya-Ya"?) Either way, I tell her, we are looking at a classic example of the genre that T. S. Eliot might have called do-not-ask-what-is-it-let-us-go-and-make-our-visit rock 'n' roll.

I explain that Miller represents a mellowed-out, bluesy sixties take on the simplistic, hyper fifties sound. That's when Emma wows me with her own profound insight. This past year her retro rock education fast-forwarded from the fifties to the sixties. She hears most of this music from movie soundtracks and TV commercials. You know, like the one where Mrs. Boomer gets Mr. Boomer to eat a high-fiber breakfast cereal to the tune of "This Is Dedicated to the One I Love."

Another song comes on, but I can't identify the artist. I know it's not Leonardo.

"Is that one of those guys who sounded like a girl?" Emma asks me. "You know, Little Somebody."

"You mean like Little Richard or Little Anthony or Little Stevie Wonder? No, this isn't Little Anybody," I explain, continuing my lecture on the fundamentals of rock.

Before I know it, Emma will be in college, and some professor of popular culture will have her writing papers like "The Inverse Relationship Between Height and Soul in Pre-Beatlean Rock."

So we ride on, the ocean below us, the mountain above us, talking about when Elvis went bad, how Three Dog Night got their name, how Paul might actually have been better than John, why Frankie Lymon never grew up and a thousand other stories. She, the budding rockomusicologist. Me, the Henry Steele Commager *cum* Dick Clark—the blathering *éminence grease.*

And with the radio blastin', goin' through it just as fast as we can now, I remember the dream I had the night before. I was in some huge auditorium filled with thousands of people all around the age of forty. We were dressed in our Sunday best—men in suits and ties, women in suits and pearls. But the behavior was strictly Juke box Saturday Night. We were all singing and swaying like a heavenly chorus.

But the hymnal was "Runaround Sue." Ten thousand well-dressed men and women singing in perfect harmony, "I said a-hey, a-hey, bumba diddy diddy. . . ."

I don't know why rock 'n' roll became the major religious experience of my generation. I don't know why we'll always love Frankie Lymon and Elvis Presley and John Lennon even if they were sick people and died or were killed before we could save them.

I do know that this music was the way millions of us —raised to be uptight middle-class marshmallows—experienced rhythm. And that was no small experience. As Lenny Bruce said, "You don't mind dying if you've got a natural sense of rhythm."

So we're riding along on this beautiful day on this beautiful highway, and this song comes on and I say to my beautiful fourteen-year-old daughter what I have said about a hundred other songs. "Emma, this was my favorite song when I was fourteen."

Then we both start singing "Shaboom" together and I think: Maybe it is all a dream, sweetheart.

When Grandma
Was a Transvestite

Sometimes years go by and miles get traveled before you can learn who you really are. It was on one of those urban evenings here on the cutting edge of civilization that I came to appreciate my bizarre heritage.

We were sitting around after dinner—my family, my friends Judy and Dobby and their little girl, Lily, and my niece Deena, visiting from Chicago.

"San Francisco is a great town for meeting men," said Deena, not realizing that she was going against the prevailing wisdom. Deena had flown in for a whirlwind weekend of Nine, DNA and a bunch of other trendy clubs those of us who sleep at night never see.

We explained to Deena the old bromide about men in San Francisco: Water, water everywhere and not a drop is straight.

"Perhaps she got lucky," allowed Dobby, an English professor, as he launched into a discussion of that dated expression. Dobby's the kind of intellectual who has theories about phrases such as "get lucky."

"You'd be surprised about San Francisco," said Deena, a worldly twenty-four-year-old. "You know how Grandma was always coming to that transvestite bar in San Francisco to meet men."

"What?" I shouted. I knew that my mother (also known as Fonzo) had, in the last decade of her life, indulged in something of a merry widowhood, but I never really appreciated the woman's perspicacity.

Deena then launched into a tale from the family legend book about the time Fonzo got the prime seat in Finocchio's, San Francisco's old drag club, by claiming she was a transvestite named Ramona.

What was it like growing up with someone as weird as Grandma Fonzo (aka Ramona), my niece wondered. I had to admit that when placed alongside my father, Grandpa Silkie, nobody even noticed Grandma Fonzo's eccentricities.

See, when you're married to a man who shakes hands with his pinkie and introduces himself as "The Silk Shirt Kid," you have to go pretty far to seem unusual.

Recently, an aunt who moved to San Francisco from Chicago shed some light on Silkie. "He did have his phobias," Aunt Charlotte said. "He always thought someone was out to get him."

"Any basis for that?" I inquired casually.

"Well, he did run that gambling operation for the Mafia in the twenties."

Against that background, I viewed Fonzo as a virtual model of decorum. But when my father died, Fonzo finally started to come into her own as an outrage.

She began her career as a lingerie saleswoman, and loved to regale us with stories of men who would come into the shop to buy the sweetie a present and say, "I'd like some undies *this big*. . . ." She would illustrate this by holding her hands in the bun-grasping position.

In college, while other girls got chocolate chip cookies from home, I would get endless CARE packages of black and red lace garments that looked as if they came from Frederick's of Hollywood instead of Mom's of Chicago.

But Fonzo's real passion was selling underwear to

oddballs. Transvestites were her favorite. She had a real talent for keeping a straight face as they explained their special needs.

I suppose it should come as no shock, then, that she might enjoy being a queen for a day herself. "What exactly was her man-meeting technique?" I asked my niece.

"I don't know, but it was probably different than mine," Deena allowed.

Deena's technique was simplicity itself. She walked up to the best-looking man in the club and said, "You're really good-looking."

Flattery, an old standby for men, now serving women.

Still, it's one thing to find an available man in San Francisco who likes women, but—a looker? "Simple," my niece explained. "When you're on vacation, you do things you wouldn't do at home."

At home, she might make passes at an ugly guy. But here, she shrugged, why not try for the jackpot?

"Look at Grandma," Deena said. "She had no trouble meeting men in San Francisco, although admittedly she might not have done the Ramona thing back home."

There are some family secrets that never come out, though. Deena could not answer the question posed by Professor Dobby:

Did Grandma, disguised as a transvestite, get lucky?

Where Have You Gone, Joe Geronimo?

One of the hardest parts of watching your kids grow up is seeing them leave a particularly charming phase. There are some moments that even your camcorder can't preserve.

Like other mothers, I'd never want to return to those thrilling days of infant colic. The terrible twos is a territory I'll gladly not revisit. But I would happily turn back the clock to when my daughter Hannah was three and had not just *one* imaginary playmate but a whole imaginary social scene.

The crowd included a man named John Shelton, who took Hannah to museums; a woman named Cindy Helleson, who went with them; and an outdoorsman named Fred DeForrest. These were the adults. But there were also the kids—Deedee and Jonathan—and their imaginary pet dog, Poopoo.

Except for the dog, the etymology of these characters eluded the rest of the family. Years after the introduction of Fred DeForrest, someone remembered that once, on a camping trip when Hannah was around two, we had been helped with a flat tire by a forest ranger named Fred.

I had also forgotten that during her fourth year, Hannah herself was an imaginary dog named Snuffy.

The whole cast of characters was recalled recently in

the offices of Joseph Wampler, kiddie dentist. Hannah and I were seated with other anxious mothers and children awaiting the dread call to the inner chamber. Your modern, enlightened kiddie dentist seats his clients en masse like a barber, hoping that group pressure will prevent anyone from freaking out. It works well except for the occasional episode of mass hysteria.

The tension in Dr. Wampler's waiting room was so thick that you could bite it with a lateral incisor. Those who were building block towers on the floor soon wrecked them with extreme gusto. Those communing with invisible companions did so with reckless abandon.

Finally, the office lady began calling out the names of the intended victims. "Amy Schultz, Jason Gordon, LeToya Roberts, Samantha and Danielle Reinis . . ." And then she said, "Snuffy—Snuffy Kahn . . ." Everybody laughed. Hannah and I looked at each other strangely.

I suddenly remembered that at the time of her initial visit, five years ago, Hannah was inhabited by Snuffy. When I filled out her medical history form, there was a question about whether the child had any nicknames. That's how the name on her chart got to be Hannah/ Snuffy Kahn.

This incident triggered a discussion of what the heck ever happened to John Shelton, Cindy Helleson and the rest of the gang. "Cindy Helleson is working as a cook at the Hard Rock Cafe London," Hannah told me without hesitation.

It was time to update the bios of the significant imaginary others: "Deedee is in junior high . . . Jonathan's in the sixth grade . . . John Shelton took a hike . . . Fred DeForrest is in the city, enjoying the views . . . Poopoo died and was replaced by a white French poodle named Fifi. . . ."

I wished I could account with that much certainty for the whereabouts of Picklepuss and Joe Geronimo.

Those two were last seen in Chicago in 1950. They were the creations of me and my sister, Myrna. They generally made their appearance when people walked by our apartment building. I would scream out the window, "Oh no, Picklepuss." Then Myrna would yell, "Joe Geronimo!" and we would duck and laugh. We found this even funnier than leaving a purse filled with mud on the sidewalk and watching passersby open it.

Occasionally, we would select strangers at random from the phone book and repeat the Joe Geronimo scenario. I have no idea now why Myrna and I found this dialogue incredibly hilarious—milk-through-the-nose hilarious. Nor can I explain how our imaginary friends came and went from our lives.

Somewhere out there in Pretendsville, the Picklepusses and the Fred DeForrests and the Deedees and the late Poopoos must surely be wondering what ever happened to all the real people they used to know.

Stress Reduction for Seven-Year-Olds

We were standing at the bus stop, we mothers of detention, waiting to send our children off to the slammer of summer day camp. Before the day was over, we would have on our conscience a day of enforced singing, hiking, nature study and—yes—lanyard making.

This camp, Camp Kee Tov, is operated by a synagogue, which does not mean that the camp features religious activities. We parents try to keep prayer out of the camps and the schools and on TV where it belongs.

These days, just as little Jewish and Moslem children attend YMCA camps, little Christians and Buddhists arrive in their Camp Kee Tov T-shirts with the familiar logo—pine trees and the Star of David.

It is a popular camp because it is well run, overprotective and—you know what they say about Jewish camp counselors—they don't beat the kids.

Now most kids are happy to be going to this camp because it's better than sixty straight days of "Days of Our Lives." But apparently some kids just can't handle it. On the third day of camp, I heard two mothers talking as they loaded their little darlings on the bus.

"Where's your older son, Jesse?" asks Mom No. 1.

"Oh, he's not coming," says Mom No. 2. "He's taking a mental-health day."

A mental-health day! On the third day of day camp?

And what exactly does a mental-health day for a seven-year-old consist of?

Let's see. We begin with a breakfast in bed of Fruit Loops and Squeezit. Squeezit is the hot new cold drink from that nice, reassuring Betty Crocker lady. You suck it out of a pink plastic bottle, so it's kind of like nursing off a Beverly Hills mother. And, as it says on the label, "Kids love the taste of new Squeezit! Each delicious flavor contains 10% real fruit juice."

After breakfast, it's time for an hour of indoor skateboard therapy. That's where little Jesse skateboards back and forth into the walls, letting out all those nasty aggressions that prevent him from being the best Jesse he can.

This is followed by several hours of prerecorded cartoons. By identifying with powerful half-human, half-Lego animated psychopaths with names like Rebar and Turgor, Jesse finds his self-esteem renewed.

The afternoon will include an emergency visit to his child psychologist, a seven-year-old like himself, who wears a suit and a fake beard and agrees with Jesse, "Your mom and dad are swine."

On the way home, Mom stops at McDonald's drive-through—Jesse can't handle the scene inside. After checking for drive-through shootings, he purchases a Happy Meal, eating only the fries and Coke and casting his McNuggets to the wind.

Returning home, Mom sets up the VCR with "Smurfs," "Gummi Bears" and "Alvin and the Chipmunks." Mom fears that "Pee-wee's Playhouse" may trigger latency fantasies. But not to worry. As soon as she is out of the room, Jesse switches on "Santa Barbara" to see if Cruz is bagging Eden.

Everyone needs a mental-health day now and then, and this one worked. The next morning Jesse was at the bus stop relaxed and refreshed. He was ready to sing, to explore nature and to weave a lanyard. "How do you feel?" his concerned mother asks as the bus arrives. Renewed, he answers, "I'm ready to kick butt."

Rebel with a Tapered Cause

I guess I started in on her about thirteen years ago, on the day she was born. "Someday, my dear daughter," I said, looking into her glistening baby eyes, "someday you will be a teenager and you will rebel against me and say cruel things you don't mean and make my life as much fun as a prison guard's. . . ."

"No, Mama, no. I'll love you forever," the goo-goo face seemed to say. "I am your monster. I will do your bidding."

And so the years went by, I reminding her daily, "This is going to turn sour." She, by her every deed and word, was a devoted monster, doing my bidding.

Then, just about the time I began to believe we would defy the Mother-Girl Programmable Curse—whammo! Teenage daughter from the pits of hell.

I suppose I should say that one reason I was so certain that things would turn ugly was my own teenage rebellion. Without going into too much detail about what I did to my mother, let's just say I had the woman walking around talking to herself, begging me to eat a meal at home.

You know you've got a parent disciplined when you step out on a religious holiday saying, "I'm going to the schoolyard to play strip poker with the boys and you can't stop me. . . ."

Plus, I was not alone in my rebellion. I was part of a big, fat, sassy generation that wrote the book on rebellion. Or at least the screenplay. We cut our wisdom teeth on James (Rebel Without a Cause) Dean and Marlon (Wild One) Brando.

"What are you rebelling against?" the waitress asks Brando in the archetypal scene.

"What have you got?" he responds.

Around the age when previous generations had to grow up, get a job, get a haircut, my generation hit the late sixties. A reprieve. Whole new opportunities to torture our parents as we moved into our twenties. Jobs were for wage slaves. Growing up was for straights. Haircuts were for plastic people. We had a mass case of terminal coolness.

Then we had kids, and the party was over. "Just wait until you have kids," our parents had said smugly, and now we know why.

But having tried every form of rebellion ourselves, we assume the I'm-so-hip-they-can't-fool-me position toward our kids. That's what today's new, sensitive parents talk about: What are the latest trends in rebellion? What have we left for them?

What our kids love to do is look at pictures of their parents when they were hippies and point and laugh. You'll see them getting out the family album with their friends, and somebody will howl, "Look at those bell-bottoms!" followed by the kind of group laughter and choking that we knew only when we were seeking higher consciousness.

Here is how they're rebelling: ankle-tight jeans. Guess? jeans. They are the antithesis of bell-bottoms. By wrapping virtual tourniquets around their legs, they are making a statement about how stupid they think we looked.

But we are old and wise. We have seen fads come and go. We have seen Marilyn in and Marilyn out. We have seen the rise and fall of the American hemline. We have seen ponytails go on women and come back on men at least twice.

So I have the following bet with my daughter. We will have lunch on New Year's Day 2000. If she hasn't worn bell-bottoms by then, I'll pay. But if she has, she has to pay.

I plan to eat a lot.

Although she is certain she will win, there are already signs of weakening. Yesterday she came in and said, "I might want to get a tie-dyed shirt." I began laughing.

"Not an ugly-hippie-rainbow Grateful Dead one," she insisted, "a single-color pretty one."

It's the beginning of the end. Soon, she'll be wearing pants with cuffs like a mermaid's fins. Time, time, time is on my side. See you at Chez Expensive, sweetheart.

Art Is
Dog Spelled Backwards

We were going to see art, ready or not.

We were Mrs. Gorton's second-grade class at Oxford School.

Mrs. Gorton was preparing us for the experience.

"We are going to an art museum," she said. "You may see some things there that will surprise you. Sometimes artists paint old people with wrinkles; sometimes they paint horses; sometimes they make statues of people with their heads off, and sometimes they paint people with their clothes off. I don't want any snickering or giggling if you see a girl or a woman or a man with clothes off."

I looked at my daughter Hannah, and we both bit our lips.

"How many of you have looked in the mirror?" she continued. "How many of you can look at a statue with clothes off without being silly?"

Everyone in the second grade raised his or her little hand. I, a chaperone, a grown-up, a mirror-looker, the beneficiary of several decades of self-actualization . . . I knew better. I might—I just might—get silly.

There was a wild, exuberant run to the school bus to begin our journey. Fortunately, we were in the hands of Cecil—the most awesome and respected driver in the district. He took no art from anyone.

"Put that toy away or I'll throw it out the window," Cecil told one budding aesthete.

Next we were taking BART to art. On the train, one big boy was giving me a hard time. "Give him a minus point," someone urged. When he sat on his friend's lap and leaned against an innocent passenger, I said sternly, "OK, that's a minus point."

Suddenly, he began to sob. "Everybody always picks on me."

"I'm sorry," I said. What could I do? Buy him a drink?

As we were about to enter the Oakland Museum, Brandon begged me to let him stay outside and look at the fish in the pond. I explained that we had to stay together.

"But I hate art," he said. "I love nature."

A couple of years in New York City and we could straighten that boy out.

Wide-eyed and innocent, we entered the special exhibit hall to see the Robert Arneson retrospective.

"This looks like dog dookie," one boy shouted.

It was not a critical assessment; it was an accurate description of a favorite theme of the artist.

There were none of the naked people Mrs. Gorton had warned us about. We had no reason to snicker.

"Here's some more scat," shouted another boy.

"That's short for scatological leavings," Mrs. Gorton explained. "We learned that from Ranger Tim at the park."

It was hard to enforce a sense of proper decorum, of respect for the dignity of art, in the presence of an artist who created huge portraits of himself with his fingers in his nose.

Kailin, Lonnel and Alex started break-dancing in the corner. Other kids started shouting, "Look at this! Look

186 - ALICE KAHN

at this!" They were getting into it. The artist was speaking to them. The guards looked nervous.

Everyone gathered around one self-portrait, a statue of Arneson with grotesque details right down to his hairy belly. Even though he had most of his clothes on, it was difficult not to be silly around that masterpiece. One even suspected that the artist was seeking silliness.

Heather observed, "He looks like Madonna's grandfather."

Tanninha pointed to the Twinkies engraved in the pedestal holding the bust of George Moscone. I treated them to the simple version of the Dan White story: "He said the Twinkies made him do it." The rest of us may have found that implausible, but it was something those seven-year-olds could relate to.

Finally, we were taken into the museum's main collection and led around by docents. When we broke into small groups, the kids really got into the art experience, shouting out their thoughts and questions and opinions. It was a dramatic illustration of the value of small class size.

Katherine Hunt, our fantastic docent, stopped by an old California scene of a bear hunt. "Why do you think they killed him?" she asked. "Food," said Arika. "Clothing," said Evan. Finally, a thoughtful boy named Ben spoke up. "Insulation?" he asked.

When it was time to leave, the children bolted the museum as charged up on art as they might be on Twinkies. Out on the street a boy pointed to some dog scat. "Art," he said.

You Can't Teach an Old Moon New Tricks

Of all the burger joints in all of the towns, why did he have to walk into mine?

He is the man in the moon, the singing crescent in shades, the guy in the McDonald's commercial who sings, "When the clock strikes—*yeah!*—half past six, *babe* . . ." He is known as Mac Tonight. Looking vaguely like a plastic heroin addict, he is Marketing Research's latest scientific discovery.

Well, he isn't the actual animated cartoon. He is some poor slob in a huge, white molded moon head being paid to walk around and shake his booty.

Actually, I knew that out of 7,500 McDonald's, he was coming to this one in Albany, California. But I couldn't stay away. I'm a mass-experience freak.

Today the joint is packed. Everyone has balloons with drawings of a pirate, leftovers of some previous corporate creature who failed to win hearts and bucks.

A crowd of thirteen-year-old skateboarders in Spuds McKenzie T-shirts is waiting out in front. Will Mac Tonight be the next Spuds McKenzie, the next Speedy Alka-Seltzer, the next Charlie the Star-Kist Tuna, the next Buster Brown, the new Dancing Raisin? Or will he be consigned to that fly-by-night hell of singing washing machines and dancing toilet bowls? Are we watching the birth or death of an icon?

Does the moon have legs?

I am with my daughter Hannah and her friend Lily. "Are you going to write about this? Will you quote me?" asks Hannah, trying to cash in on the Kahn Child Exploitation Buyout Law—you get five bucks if quoted. A Happy Meal is not enough these days.

Hannah is my deep source, my stethoscope on the heartbeat of pop culture. I know that Mac Tonight is what's hot because for weeks Hannah has been walking around doing impressions of Mac, singing, like Bobby Darin, "Come on, baby, make it Mac Tonight. . . ."

I try to tell her how I saw the real Bobby Darin, backstage at the Chez Paree nightclub in Chicago, 1959. He had Frank Sinatra-ized Kurt Weill's haunting song about Mackie Messer and had the No. 1 hit. I entered the club with a fake ID, but the bartender wouldn't serve me the pink lady I ordered.

That wasn't my biggest disappointment. After the show, my girlfriend and I rushed backstage to get Bobby Darin's autograph. He was loaded and had a babe on each arm. He gave me a boozy kiss and handed me a glossy of himself. He was smaller than life.

Hannah and Lily aren't interested in history. Outside our McWindow, a '59 pink Caddie convertible is pulling up. "It's the Mac Tonight dude!" says Hannah.

He gets out and dances through the outlet while a DJ follows him with a ghetto blaster playing the twice-bastardized Kurt Weill song over and over. Everyone rushes to shake his gloved hand. Just like Bobby Darin, he hands them pictures of himself.

Four-year-old Ashley Green jumps into her mother's arms screaming, "I want to go home."

Nancy Hayden of Gelman & Gray/Lowry Communications, a San Francisco PR agency, set up the 16-McDonald's Bay Area tour after test-marketing in L.A.

I asked Hayden if Mac's ascendancy represents a threat to Ronald McDonald. "Oh no," she insists. "Ronald McDonald is the second most identifiable children's character, after Santa Claus."

Mac Tonight goes through the Albany outlet again. He has to stay there for an hour. By the third go-round, few people are left who want to touch him. He goes into the kitchen, trying to find someone to pay attention to him. He might as well be just another McNugget. He's getting smaller than life.

Santa Claus may not be worried. But over at the agency that handles him, Ronald McDonald's people are breathing a sigh of relief.

"He's got to get more tricks," says Lily.

"He's got to get his act together," says Hannah.

The truth is, he's only a plastic moon sailing over a Styrofoam sea.

The Swinging Single Life with Kids

Remember the antique notion of staying together for the kids? You know, when Harriet thought she was going to puke if she had to look at Ozzie just one more time, but she maintained for the sake of the boys. Or when Robert (Knows Best) Young would be lying there in his twin bed across the room from Jane (Knows Nothing) Wyatt, dreaming of Mamie Van Doren but not acting on his impulses because he dare not wreck the idyllic lives of Bud, Kitten and Princess.

Around the time Lucy told Desi to take his conga and shove it, millions of other Americans came to the conclusion that they did not have to endure a living hell until the kids were grown. Divorce rates skyrocketed.

Today, almost as many kids live in single-parent homes as in two-parent homes. Sociologists are still divided on the effects on the child of living in a one-parent home—other than a much greater chance of poverty.

But has anybody studied the effects on the parent of raising a kid alone?

I start from the premise that raising kids even under the best of circumstances is the most difficult thing a person can attempt. It's my belief that the reason men have always worked outside the home and women are now doing it in record numbers is so that no one has to take the rap for the walking disaster who at age twenty starts running up a huge shrink bill.

"Blame the nanny," scream her parents. "We were both at work."

If Freud were alive today, he'd have to come up with the Sourpuss Complex. That's where you want to kill your mother and marry your *au pair* girl.

One of the most disturbing trends in popular mythology today is the sitcom view of single fathering. *Three Men and a Baby*, a box-office smash, and the popular TV shows "My Two Dads" and "Full House" are all *fun* looks at men raising children alone. They seem to start from the paranoid fantasy that since women are now working, they will abandon their children to the men. And—the fantasy continues—since men are such natural devoted mothers, there's no problem.

Throw Momma from the train. Who needs her?

Never mind that the number of children abandoned by their mothers is minuscule compared with the number abandoned by Dad. It's the unusual that makes for a funny "concept," as they say in L.A. But what I find truly disturbing in these comedies is the idea that single parenting is funny.

For the past five days, my husband has been away on business. My days have become an Olympic obstacle course. Let's look at yesterday:

Wake up at seven. Read four newspapers. Get younger daughter ready for school. Try to persuade her to eat something other than potato chips for breakfast. Make sure she has lunch, ear-infection medicine and homework. Drive her to school.

Come home. Realize elder daughter is sick and wants room service. Drive to grocery store. Bring her tray with tulips, croissant and orange. (Tulips were on sale.) Call her doctor, call her school, call younger daughter's after-school program to cancel.

Write column.

Go to open house to check out next year's school.

Get embarrassed when other mother says, "I pulled over when I saw you driving like a maniac to get here."

Race back home to get elder daughter and take her to doctor for throat culture.

Pick up younger daughter. Rent *Indiana Jones*. Work on column. Call editor. Plead for his sympathy.

Call summer program for kids. Discover it is too late to apply. Throw together horrible junk-food dinner. Feel guilty. Make kids do homework. Fight with kids. Hug and kiss kids.

Get in bed. Realize I have forgotten to pay bills, brush teeth, take out garbage, exercise, read more, comb hair and reduce stress.

Feel lonely. Call husband. His day: breakfast, twelve hours of work, dinner in hotel room, sleep.

Pray husband comes back. Understand why June Cleaver was ready to be Ward Cleaver's love slave.

Tough Guys Don't Squirm in the Jewelry Store

My daughters are growing up in the postfeminist era. When a guy comes on TV talking about how it's OK to hit a woman as long as you use an open hand, nobody has to teach them what to do. They were born knowing how to hiss. They just tighten their teeth and blow.

When they see a panel of men discussing an important issue on TV, they will instinctively ask, "Why aren't there any girls?" They didn't need to go to consciousness-raising sessions. They didn't need a class in Women's Herstory. They've never even read a single self-esteem book.

And since nobody ever told them that girls aren't supposed to be good at certain things, the older daughter passed me at math when she was nine, and the younger daughter could outrun me almost as soon as she could outwalk me.

When young jock Hannah, nine, and I were riding past a park the other day, I commented on the scene. "Isn't that nice?" I said. "It's a boy and a dad playing baseball."

She was apparently born with the sarcasm gene and said mockingly, "Oh yes, a boy and a dad—how very nice. Why is it always a boy and a dad? A girl and a dad playing baseball would be nice. A girl and a mom playing soccer would be better."

Being a postfeminist mom isn't easy, especially if you were raised to be a prefeminist klutz. But consider the plight of the postfeminist boy. This brave new role was on exhibit recently in our neighborhood earring store.

I had long ago abandoned my stand against the girls getting their ears pierced. I knew it was a hopelessly old-fashioned attitude on my part, and after throwing out a few lighthearted comments about "primitive mutilation rituals," I took my older daughter to the doctor when she was eleven for a sixty-dollar sterile-technique piercing. When she was a little older, she came home and announced that she had gotten a "double pierce" for free from a hippie selling earrings on the street.

The second daughter, benefiting from her sister's pioneer work and community trends, got her ears done at an earring store this year. (After all, Samantha and Danielle and Sarah and Lily all had theirs done.) When she lost all her earrings and the holes closed up, I sprang for a second mutilation ritual last week, keeping my opinions to myself.

In the shop was a man with his nine-year-old son. Both of them were dressed in conventional T-shirts, jeans and boots. If the son had any trouble convincing his dad that all the cool young dudes had pierced ears, there was no sign of the struggle. The dad paid his non-refundable sixteen dollars for the birthstone stud, the antiseptic and the piercing procedure. He signed the release absolving the store from blame should his son die in the cause of trend-following.

However, when the shop clerk went to shoot him in the ear, the boy began to squirm. After several tries, he refused. "I can't do it," he cried out. The father attempted to reason with him. "Look, Jason, we can't get our money back. Now sit still and take your earring like a man."

He actually said that. Can you imagine what he'll say when Jason tries to walk in high heels? "Don't wince, boy. Remember you're a Walton."

But Jason was squirming and appeared close to tears. So my Hannah went ahead of him. It was almost as if she were saying: "Well, I'll show this boy how to hang tough at a piercing." She sat perfectly still and took it. Like a girl.

Now the father looked truly humiliated. I tried to console him. "Boys aren't raised to suffer for fashion," I said. He didn't seem consoled.

Hannah stood there right next to Jason, saying, "It doesn't hurt, really." Jason didn't seem convinced.

Finally, Jason's father took him to a corner of the store for a serious dressing-down. I imagined his saying things like, "You get that earring or I'm gonna whup your hide, boy."

I said to my daughter, "Maybe he's afraid he'll cry when it happens. We should leave." Not wanting to witness such an ugly scene, Hannah left, looking proud.

I'm sure she pondered the essential mystery of modern life. How can boys be so good at baseball but such sissies at earrings?

The Aging Dork and Her She-Monster

You know the old Lenny Bruce line about Doberman pinschers—"Ya love 'em, ya feed 'em: twelve years later they kill you." I've been thinking about this ever since my daughter turned thirteen.

I keep going back over the good old days. When she was one and only drooled and smiled. When she was in nursery school and would wear only frilly dresses. The intellectual years, ages eight to ten. And now, this creature from junior high, this she-monster from the hormonitorium.

Among the shared lore of parenting are various opinions on the age at which kids are at their worst. Interestingly, you can find a parent with a child of any age eager to offer that age for tops in the misery derby.

Common wisdom frequently nominates thirteen as the worst age for girls. (But when I tell people my kid is thirteen, they say, "It's only going to get worse"—a truly frightening thought.) Boys at five, sixteen and thirty-three are supposed to be hell. Both sexes are said to stink at two, and we're not just talking diapers.

My grocery clerk volunteered twenty-two. "Twenty-two is definitely the worst age," he said as he packed my potato chips, Popsicles and Pepperidge Farm Milanos. (Milanos are "hell of icy," in case you didn't know.)

"How old is your kid?" I asked him.

"Twenty-two," he said.

My husband and I take turns being the rational one in dealing with this thirteen-year-old *situation*. I, for example, stopped him the other day. He was preparing his response to the third lost key and second lost bus pass in less than a month.

"I'm going to tell her that she has to be more responsible," he said. "That if she expects grown-up privileges, she has to show grown-up behavior. And . . . that her irresponsible, slovenly attitude is the reason America is going down the tubes."

"Skip the part about America," I coached him.

A few days later, I blew up at her when I found all those valuable clothes she *had* to have lying balled up in a corner of her closet. These are things I would never buy for myself except on sale. In fact, I now wait for her to tire of her clothes so I can get them. Hand-me-ups, I call them. It's the only way I'll ever get an Esprit sweater.

"Try to talk to her about her ideas for a change, instead of her behavior," the husband calmly advised.

"Ideas?" I asked him. "What ideas? You mean like Descartes and eyeliner?"

It is unfortunate for my daughter that she seems to have one of the more suspicious and nosy mothers in town. I am what gets called overprotective in the eighties. That means that I want to know whom she's with, what she's doing and whether there will be any adults around. I try to explain my concerns to my daughter. They start with weapons and assault, then drift down to drugs.

I try to explain that I was once a crazy thirteen-year-old, but that in the olden days nobody was armed and stoned.

I suppose it's too much to expect that she'll understand a mother's fears. Kids will tell you to just relax. If you walk around at night, no harm can come to you if you're in groups of four. And even if no adults are at the party, there's nothing to worry about because somebody's older brother will be in the house.

Parents are such dorks. They can imagine four crazed maniacs going after four crazed girls. And a teenage boy is not a parent's idea of a great chaperone. A teenage boy is the person who buys the wine cooler, not the person who tells you to stop drinking it.

Kids come back with the final appeal to community standards: How come the Other Kids can always do everything?

I tell my daughter that I love her and that it's my job to protect her until she's twenty-one. She tells me that my overprotectiveness is ruining her social life.

That's the idea.

five

The

DAY I

DROVE the

DISK

DRIVE

DOWN

I'm the Number on Dustin Hoffman's Dashboard

It happened last spring when I was sitting at my computer, determined to bring in my column on time and under budget. I had turned down the answering machine, but it was still audible enough to hear a voice say, "I'm calling for Dustin Hoffman. Mr. Hoffman would like to speak to you. . . ."

You may wonder how I could keep a thing like my relationship with Dustin a secret from you. But I figured if I went babbling, no one would believe me.

Then I went to see *Rain Man*, with Hoffman's fine portrayal of the autistic Raymond Babbitt, and it all came back. You see, it was *Rain Man* that took Dustin away from me.

At the time of the first phone call, the reflex that says "I'm only in for Hoffman, Brando and Jesus Christ" instinctively grabbed the phone. I immediately understood why famous people call ahead to let you know they're going to be calling. It gives you a couple of hours to untie your tongue.

Generally, I hate to do stories about celebrities. You quickly realize you've got either a beautiful, well-trained animal on your hands or someone who is much smarter and more manipulative than you are. There's no way you can have a relationship between equals. For journalism's sake, I usually pretend I'm Barbara Walters and say things like, "Tell me about your pain, Sly. . . ."

But then Dustin himself called me. Why? The scratchy Ratso Rizzo voice on the car phone explained that he had seen me on a TV show called "Women on Sex." The show had been taped months earlier for the Playboy channel, although I had never seen it. In it, I and University of Washington sociologist Dr. Pepper Schwartz were having an intellectual discussion about "Mating Habits of the North American Yuppie."

In between my nervous giggles and the sounds of Los Angeles traffic, I heard Dustin say that I talked out of the corner of my mouth, that I took everything in and "Cuisinarted" it out, that his wife, Lisa, and his children enjoyed the show and that Lisa thought he should call and let me know this. We talked some more about life, relationships and sex roles.

"I usually talk to people who've seen me in movies," he said. "But I've seen you on television, so we already share a voyeuristic relationship."

Wow.

Unfortunately, I had to pick up my daughter from school. He said he would call me back. "Tell your wife she's a real prince," I told him.

"Tell your husband he's a real princess," he responded.

My exact notes from the conversation read: "Corner. Everything coming in—Cuisinarted. Nichols and May. Wife Lisa. As Paddy Chayefsky said." That's how cogent I was.

When my daughter came in from school and realized that I had been talking to the actor who was about to make a movie with Tom Cruise, she said, "Tell him to get me Tom Cruise's autograph."

"I don't think you understand," I told her. "I can't

ask him to do that. He's a great actor. A legend . . . an artist."

"So get his autograph, too."

I guess I was pretty star-struck myself because when I woke up the morning after the phone call, my husband looked at me and said, "Dustin: Day Two."

The phone calls continued over the next few weeks. I listened as Dustin drove around Los Angeles and talked to me about life as if I were a . . . well, a person. It was just like talking to one of my best friends. He was funny, hip and weird.

He described the physical exam they made him take before *Rain Man*. He told me how his doctor reassured him of the simplicity of a proctological exam by taking one alongside him. (This obviously is not a service the doctor provides for anyone below the A list.) He told me Oprah Winfrey jokes. He mentioned—what else?—a project. He told me stuff he learned while researching the life of Lenny Bruce. Stuff Shecky told him about Frank.

He had his people call my people (who were me). When I returned one of his phone calls, I got one of his people who said, "I could lose my job for saying this, but he is kind of like the character in *Rain Man*. He's brilliant, but he starts lots of things and then forgets them. Kind of an idiot savant himself."

I guess my disappointment came through the wires because that was when the assistant said, "But your number is at the top of his dashboard."

I missed another call, and that was it. He went off to make *Rain Man* instead of my day.

When we came out of the theater after seeing the movie, my daughter looked at me with venom in her eyes and said, "You could have gotten their autographs."

Meanwhile, I was updating my résumé, trying to figure out what all this could mean to my career:

1965—B.A. English Lit.
1973—B.S. Nursing
1988—Number at the top of Dustin Hoffman's
dashboard.

The Bicoastal Network
Hot-Line Trend

I was sitting around with my husband and my 2.5 children, drinking my 1.5 glasses of wine. Suddenly, the phone rang. It was another urgent call for the Trends Hot Line.

On the phone was my old friend Allen Fletcher, now working as a newspaper reporter in Worcester, Massachusetts.

"Hi, how's your career?" asked Allen—the eighties version of "What's happening, baby?"

"Fine, thanks, and yours?" I said—the subtle way of asking, "Can you do anything for me or do you want something from me?"

"I just got an assignment from my editor to write about what life will be like in Worcester in 1992, based on what's going on in California now. He figures that whatever's happening there now will be here in a few years. So, what's happening there? What's hot and what's not?"

Under the influence of my 1.5 glasses, I had no problem coming up with facts—true or not. A few days later, I called Allen and told him I was doing a column on my friend from Worcester calling to ask me the latest trends. Would he please read his notes, I asked, so I could remember what the hell I'd said.

And just like that, a personal phone call became two pieces of serious journalism.

My first reaction to Allen's query had been: "Car shades." Since Allen had never seen one, he assumed I was putting him onto something major.

"Careers are very big, too," shouted my husband from the peanut gallery.

"How about food?" Allen asked. "What's happening in the chic world of Bay Area food?"

"Pot roast," I said without a moment's hesitation. "Home cooking . . . major trend."

"Are you telling me people are eating at home there?" he asked.

"No," I said. "We're going to restaurants with lace curtains and fireplaces for pot roast."

"You mean jet-setters will be flying into Worcester for pot roast?"

"Get out your awning," I advised.

I also told him that seventies nostalgia was really hot. "What was the seventies?" he asked, reasonably enough. Some people who lived through it apparently hardly noticed.

"You know, pointy-collared, polyester print shirts, hideous clothes. The Eagles, America, Fleetwood Mac, 'Sweet Judy Blue Eyes'—Dadadot da-da dotdot da-da. . . ."

Allen then formulated his thesis. He speculated that since Worcester, culturally, had just reached 1975, if the seventies were back, then Worcester was totally In.

"Yes," I said, "but do you have minimalism, nihilism and retro? You need these things to be In." What do *they* know about In-ness out there?

"What's retro?" he asked.

"Looking backward," I explained.

"We got it!" he shouted. "What else do we need?"

"You need bread," I said. "Bread is very big here—we've got designer bakeries. We've also got single-malt scotch, blue-corn tortillas and Belgian endive. Oh yes, putting down drugs while still using them is very popular."

"What else do you got? What else is hot?"

I was on a roll. *I* was hot. "We've got homelessness, kidnapping your own kids, Kris Kristofferson—stupidity is always very big—and everything you saw on that TV show 'Amerika' is here right now.

"Manipulation of people is always hot. Right now, remote control as a concept is very big."

The husband began shouting out his usual cheerful predictions. "Return of the oil crisis. Arabs back in control. Mounting AIDS deaths . . ."

"Ignore him," I suggested. "Let's get serious. The outdoors is out." But I couldn't say for sure if the indoors was In.

As we spoke, I looked out the window and saw a man walking outside. He was pacing back and forth along the block. He looked as if he was casing the house across the street. He appeared to be gesturing to another man sitting in a van.

"Paranoia is very big," I told the trend sniffer.

Soon a police car raced up the street. The walker began jogging rapidly. I knew this was worrisome in light of the fact that jogging had peaked in '85. The van turned around and sped away.

"Breaking and entering is very hot right now, and so are compact discs," I said.

"Well, thanks for the help," he said.

"No problem," I responded. "Network me anytime." Then I got off the phone and stole his story.

That's what friends are for.

Phone Zombie Torments College Prof

Crocodile Schwartz was a man of science, an engineer, a product of Stanford University. But he said something weird once that I've never forgotten.

It's been at least thirteen years since my friend Crocodile (*né* Lenny) Schwartz went off to teach math in Australia. He was an American success story. A poor boy from the Bronx who through the miracle of dynamite SAT scores came to be a professor down under.

Shortly before he faded into the outback, Lenny and I had a conversation about the New York phone system, and he said something very strange. He was talking about what a mess that phone system is. "It's totally out of control," he said. "Bizarre things happen that you wouldn't believe."

"What kind of bizarre things?" I asked.

"Oh, like phone calls from the dead."

Phone calls from the dead! To this day, I've regretted not pressing him to explain what he meant. Every time I had a strange encounter with the telephone I thought: Maybe that's what Lenny meant.

There are those routine phone calls from the dead like the machines that call to sell me something. And there are weird messages left on my phone machine like the twelve calls for a Mrs. DeGrazzio, warning her that if she does not pay up, her newspaper delivery person will cut her off. Phone calls threatening death.

One morning I picked up the phone and heard, "Hello, Alice Kahn? This is Lois Drale from the IRS. Your name came up this morning. . . ."

As my heart jumped out of my chest, I thought: Maybe Lenny meant to say phone calls that can knock you dead. Then Lois Drale continued, "We were wondering if you could speak at our annual meeting—maybe introduce a little humor to our workers. . . ."

I told her—in as polite a way as possible—to drop dead.

Lately I've been aware of a strange tendency people have to make phone calls and hope nobody is there. "Oh, it's you—live," one says, trying to conceal disappointment. "I was hoping to reach your machine." Phone calls to the dead.

But Lenny left the States before phone machines became as common as Camembert cheese. I had to know! Just what are phone calls from the dead?

I got the number of a Len Schwartz in Adelaide, Australia, but when he answered, the accent was decidedly not Bronx.

"You want the Lenny Schwartz who grew up in New York and went to school in California?" he said. "I'm a tennis pro. I been to California . . ."

G'day, mate.

Then I called the University of Adelaide switchboard. "Schwartz . . . Schwartz," said the operator. "That is an unusual name."

"Not in the Bronx," I told her.

I was finally informed that Lenny had left years ago and was now teaching at the University of Delaware in Newark, a suburb of Philadelphia. Crocodile Schwartz was actually Rocky Schwartz!

Soon I had him, alive and well and on the phone. "Yes, Alice, they pronounce it New Ark," Lenny was saying with that unmistakable Bronx accent. "This, after all, is the home of Shickhouse Franks, whose motto is: 'The most carefully pronounced hot dogs in America.' "

We talked about what had happened in the years since we'd last spoken. Two weeks before my daughter Hannah came into this world, he had twins—Joshua and Jonathan, Rocky II and Rocky III. After the obligatory *Big Chill* conversation about which old friends from our peace-march days were now running Exxon and who had made a killing in real estate, I got to my question. Just exactly what had he meant by "phone calls from the dead"?

"Oh, I suppose I was a little loose when I said it. I was just being theatrical. You know how people say the post office is so inefficient that by the time a letter arrives the sender is dead. Obviously, an inefficient phone system . . ."

I was feeling gypped. "Are you trying to tell me that after thirteen years of wondering what you meant, that nobody is, in fact, getting phone calls from the dead?"

"Well, Alice," he said, "this is pretty damn close."

The Day I Drove the Disk Drive Down

The rainy Saturday stretched before me like a 20-megabyte disk waiting to be filled. It was 9:00 A.M., and I was bored already. I'd eaten my Shredded Wheat and banana. Now . . . what to do?

The gray skies were relentless. It was the kind of weekend you wanted to delete. And then this idea popped onto my screen.

I grabbed my husband and my Visa card and headed off to the Whole Earth Access Company. Today was the day I would make the great leap forward. Today was the day I'd leave my mid-eighties mid-sized computer behind and move on up to a state-of-the-art Macintosh Plus with a hard disk drive.

Everyone who saw my little old Macintosh with its cute little external drive said, "Someone like you needs more power." People couldn't believe I was still dragging that mouse across those wimpy little floppy disks. Someone like me needed hard disks, megabytes, certainly much more power.

And I was sick of wasting my incredibly valuable time staring at the clock icon while waiting for the machine to function. I was an iconoclast. I wanted to be able to click and go.

By high noon on that rainy Saturday, with a mere flick of the Visa card, I was up 20 megabytes and out two grand.

We came home and unpacked all the boxes. The new computer, the external hard disk drive, four manuals, three simple, self-explanatory disks, cables to connect my modem, my printer, special connections for the so-called "scuzzy-port,"—hey, I was learning the lingo.

I sat there like the Queen of Oz while my husband connected the whole thing. Pay no attention to that man behind the curtain, I told myself.

"Ready," he said.

I went straight to work because time is money and money is power, and now I had more power so I ought to make more money.

The first thing I noticed was that the new hard disk drive made a horrible noise. It sounded like . . . a machine. I hate machines.

I turned it off so I could think. When I turned it back on, I couldn't get the computer to recognize the existence of the hard disk drive.

I called my husband. "Honey, I can't find my megabytes." He couldn't find them either.

I called my friend Brad. He was one of the apostles of the book *The Macintosh Bible*. But Brad wasn't home. He was at his office picking up his office computer so his kids could use his office computer at home and he could then use his home computer at home.

I read the manuals. I tried all the simple, self-explanatory disks. I clicked and double-clicked all the files. The hands of the clock icon whirled relentlessly.

Finally, I called the Whole Earth Access Company. The nice man said the drive was probably broken and that if I brought it in, they would see about getting me another one.

"How could it be broken?" I asked. "We just bought it this morning."

"Sometimes they come like that," he said. "You know, most stores won't even take things back."

The broken drive was whirling loudly. My husband said the noise wasn't the drive. It was the fan that cooled it. "It's important that you be able to hear the fan," he said, "so that you're aware of when the shit hits it."

It was hitting now.

It was four o'clock. I had wasted five hours fiddling with the damn thing. I started thinking about how I'd need a radio to cover the noise. I would need days to figure out the new computer. I could waste a lot of time on this.

We packed up the new computer, the bum drive, the four manuals, the cables and the three simple self-explanatory disks. At six o'clock, I signed the paper de-Visaing the two grand.

By seven o'clock, I was sitting in sweet silent thought, watching the clock icon on my non-state-of-the-art, nonpower computer. My friend Brad returned my call.

"I solved the problem," I told him.

"How did you do that?" he asked.

"I erased the day."

Read My Beeps

"Hi, this is my inner self. I'm not in now. . . ."

You can tell a lot about people by their phone messages.

Take my message: "This is Alice. Please leave your name, your number and your message. You can put my check in the mail."

This tells you I am a simple, no-nonsense person. And a cheap hustler.

My friend Susan has a wonderful message. "This is Susan. At the tone, please leave your name and the time and the date"—here Susan actually snickers on the tape —"and tell me about yourself."

This tells you that Susan is a journalist. She wants to know the factual details. And she cares about you. But let the caller beware. You are her potential *objet de* snickers.

My friend Jack works for the phone company. Jack lets you know that he's a now kinda guy. He has a state-of-the-art message. First you get Jack's friendly voice: "Hi, it's Jack. I can't come to the phone now because I'm in Philadelphia. But I'll be back at this number tomorrow." At the phone company you don't live in a town, you live at a number.

Then another voice comes on—the electronic lady-voice from Electronic Ladyland: "If you would like to leave a message, press 1. If you wish to speak to the operator, press 2. If you would like more options, press 3. . . ."

There are people in the Soviet Union who would die for that More Options button. And what can these options be? "If you would like to arrange a meeting with the operator, press 4. If you would like to see dirty pictures of Jack and the operator, press 5. . . ."

Sometimes you learn more about people than you would care to from their phone messages. The other day, I returned a call to a woman named Laura and got: "Hi, you've reached Laura and Steve's. Can't come to the phone now. If you wish to leave a message for Laura, please do so at the tone. As you know, Steve will be away for six months."

Well, it was news to me! I didn't know Laura and Steve were living together. I didn't even know Steve or Laura.

Once it was called "out of wedlock"; now it's called "in phone message sync." And how do Laura and Steve's mommies and daddies feel when they find out the kids are living in sync?

Maybe I'm jumping to conclusions. Maybe they're just roommates. Sure, let's go budget. One house. One fridge. One phone message. But just who does Steve think he is, walking out on her for six months like that?

Some people go to elaborate lengths to have a jazzy phone message . . . music, French accents, clever scripts. I know of one man whose friends call him periodically just to hear his latest message. Lifestyles of the Electronically Needy.

Some people work on their voice—trying to sound sexy. "Hi . . . (pant, pant, pant) . . . You have reached the offices of Ace Chemical Supply . . . (pant, pant, pant). . . ."

When I first got my phone machine, I started to record the message I'd been planning for years: "Hi, this is Alice. At the tone, please leave your name, the date, the time, your weight, your bra size, your most embarrassing moment—"

But then my daughter walked into the room and said, "Oh no! Mom, please don't try to be funny." So now when people get my brief, curt message, they always leave me this painful comment: "Hi, why aren't you funny?"

VCR Illiteracy: A National Scandal

Like millions of other Americans, I am not a slave to my technology. I'm too stupid to be. I am one of an estimated 30 million VCR illiterates. It's a national tragedy.

The same people who had brains enough not to buy a personal computer because they wouldn't know what to do with it now own VCRs that lie fallow for the same reason. And the consequences are tragic.

Hours of "Dynasty," "Who's the Boss?" and "Beauty and the Beast" are being lost to posterity—or at least until they are syndicated for rerun. A little over a year ago, we acquired a bottom-of-the-line VCR. We quickly learned to REWIND and FAST-FORWARD and soon worked our way up to SET CLOCK. But the buck stopped at EJECT.

The American dream of programming your VCR to record shows a year from next Tuesday seems to be out of the reach of the average citizen. Although I have no hard data, I'm willing to guess that at least half of all VCR owners are incapable of any tricks other than watching movies and simultaneous viewing/recording.

Certain experts place the estimate even higher. "According to some reputable source, eighty percent of all VCR owners never use their timer," says Jack Mingo.

Mingo's pretty reputable himself. As coiner of the term "couch potato" and in his official capacity as Minister of Information and Propaganda for the Couch Potato Party, Mingo shared with me his thoughts on VCR illiteracy.

"Why certainly—I'd be happy to comment on the situation, Alice, or your-name-here," Mingo told me.

"I think it's deplorable that video manufacturers have made it so difficult," he said. "Watching TV should not require a college education. It's those crazy Japanese— they follow directions, they read, they go to school. Here, we do things differently. We work with it, we play with it, and then we break it."

Toni Casal, an audio-visual production supervisor for a major corporation, is one of those who has been diddling with her VCR to no avail. She confesses that two years after purchasing their equipment, both she and her husband are incapable of operating it. Today, the Casals suffer from postpurchase depression. "We bought the seven-hundred-fifty-dollar Beta—like the professionals buy," she says. "We can't program, but we do have two remotes, and we sit there every night playing dueling remotes."

This seems pretty sophisticated to me. We have only one remote, and you have to be standing right in front of the TV to get it to work. Even then you have to keep clicking the thing and saying "shazaam," and sometimes it still doesn't work. Perhaps we should switch to "abra-cadabra."

I thought we had reached the apex of our VCR literacy when we learned to tape one program while watching another—the technological equivalent of chewing gum and tying your shoes at the same time. It's a small step, but lack of such abilities has toppled presidents.

With this technology, we are now able to watch "Wiseguy" without missing the last legs of "China Beach." Until today, I thought this was as good as modern viewing could get.

Then we met Lou Levin, the VCR maven. Lou is a one-man business: VCRs R Me. He has made it his mission in life to teach VCR wimps how to program their machines. He asks nothing in return but the recognition that he is the only real man around—a man in control of his machines. A man who is not afraid to touch knobs.

You cannot find this Johnny Programmingseed in the phone book—he finds you. Lou says teaching VCR skills has become his passion. It began a few months ago when a new love forced him into a life of monogamy, a word that for many years Lou had pronounced "monotony."

Lou says, "I used to program women; now I program VCRs."

One of the things Lou enjoys about his work is the chance to see his clients' bedrooms. He doesn't know why most people keep their VCRs there, but he enjoys going into a different bedroom every night—just for old times' sake.

I suggested to Lou that the reason we hide our VCRs in the bedroom is because we don't want to get caught with one. We regard unspontaneous TV viewing as an unnatural act. Watching "Gimme a Break" in a fit of passion is one thing. But planning ahead—this suggests deep moral weakness.

Today, thanks to the Casanova of the cassette recorder, I have the technological capability to become a full-fledged bed potato. I will soon have recordings of "Geraldo," "America's Most Wanted" and "Entertainment Tonight"—shows I'd be humiliated to watch in the originals. Lou makes no judgment on content. He's a technology freak.

But Couch Padrino Jack Mingo stresses the value of taping certain programs. " 'Gilligan's Island' is the show VCRs were made for," he says. "Only by repeated viewing will all the subtle meanings come out."

Mingo also warns that unless I store my cassettes in a lead case, just one nuclear bomb could electromagnetically zap my whole collection. He observes, "It is perhaps an unexpected side benefit of nuclear war."

Candi's Hang-up

Short of celibacy, there's no safer sex on earth than phone sex. Phone sex is a growth industry these disease-conscious days. Through the miracle of modern technology, you can reach out and not touch someone. But it has its drawbacks.

"I found the situation frustrating," says Cindi Apfel after five months of aural sex, "because I really like to talk about sex. But I was creating an identity for him, not expressing my true self."

Apfel (a pseudonym) has just ended a for-hire relationship that consisted entirely of a thirty-to-sixty-minute phone call every Friday night. She was paid ten dollars as a free-lancer for each call, regardless of length, although she had recently renegotiated the deal to fifteen dollars for forty-five minutes and twenty dollars for an hour—far less still than most phone-sex services charge.

It's obvious there's gold in them there phones, but little of the profit was coming to Candi. I asked why she didn't hang up sooner.

"I'm into a nude lifestyle," she says, "and interested in any business having to do with male and female sexuality, but . . . I have my share of hang-ups."

What hang-ups could anyone as uninhibited as Candi have? And just what is a "nude lifestyle"? She explains that it means being naked every chance you can get—at nudist colonies, at beaches, at home, in the bathtub, with friends and, if possible, at work.

"I'm an exhibitionist at some level," she admits over lunch at Scott's Seafood Grill. If she could, Candi would be sitting there in the buff attacking her coho salmon.

Instead, she sits quite obviously braless in a purple T-shirt and ankle-length denim skirt. Her strawberry-blond curly hair is partly gathered in a side ponytail tied with a purple ribbon. Her little-girlish appearance is enhanced by her gap-toothed smile, absence of makeup, wide-set blue eyes and a slow, sweet way of expressing herself.

The only clues to her true age—thirty-eight—are the lines in her face, her complex history and the thought she gives to answering my questions.

Candi has, as they say, been around the block. Besides being a phone-sex lady, she's been a nude model, a lingerie show girl, a nude bar dancer, a swingers' party escort ("I just watched") and a "boudoir photographer." Not an illogical career ladder, but something of a departure for the nice Jewish girl and Mensa member who began her adult life as an elementary school teacher.

"My mother thought being bright was the most important thing in the world. She pushed me, and I'm glad," Candi says, reflecting on her early start at college (age sixteen). "But I believe children act out their parents' repressed desires. My mother, who has a master's degree and never worked, feels under my father's thumb. I'm doing what I want, and no man is telling me what to do."

Candi considers herself a feminist. In matters erotic, she calls the shots—and that's what she feels separates a good time from pornography.

When Candi looks for roots to her exhibitionism, what she sees is her father in the backyard . . . in a bathing suit. "I'll notice myself strutting around outside in my bathing suit feeling just like him."

As I pour a second spoonful of sugar into my coffee, I look up at Candi and say, "I hope you don't mind my using this stuff."

"I've seen worse," she says.

"I'll bet you have," I reply, and we both laugh.

Her phone client initially wanted to talk "about panties," Candi says. "Well, I'm not into panties. I don't even wear underwear." But she was desperate for money, so they talked panties.

He would also call up at other times because he was lonely, just to talk. "He started calling me up separately to talk about investments and what he should do with his bank notes."

There must be a whole potential "yuppie porn" industry out there, I thought—a place where live nude investment counselors can talk of market dominance, rising interest rates, stocks and bondage.

One reason Candi thought she would like the professional phone relationship—aside from her abiding interest in "any business having to do with sexuality"—is her experience as an "amateur." She had placed personal ads for years looking for a boyfriend, and "I talked to hundreds of guys at least two hours every time."

During those long phone calls to decide whether they would meet, inevitably they'd talk sex. Doubtless the phone-sex services of the eighties grew out of the seventies boom in personal ads. Some sharp entrepreneur probably thought: Let's skip the "young-urban-professional-into-Mozart-and-ecology" part and get right down to garter belts and high heels.

"I had problems talking to my own partners about sex," Candi says. "I would get shy and too embarrassed to say what I wanted. I was looking for information on how to communicate with men. Those calls were like therapy for me."

There probably was some therapeutic benefit for the potential suitors also.

I asked Candi whether she ever talked shop with other phone-sex professionals. Do they share her dislike of the work? "I have one friend who really enjoys it," she replies, "but he's a guy who can make his voice sound like a girl."

Reached by phone, Candi's friend, Sam, told me he began disguising his voice when he was a teenager making crank calls. He said the phone-sex business has cut down on crank calls because "now people can pay and get exactly what they want."

Sam, who is straight, said he learned a lot about men from the phone business. "Most of these guys want acceptance—to be told they're OK," he said. "I had one guy who would get excited by somebody snapping their fingers."

He said many "dominance calls" come from executives. "These are guys who are in power all day and want relief, so they'd call and ask me to tell them what to do." Sam liked to tell them to bark like a dog. "To hear a guy go 'woof, woof' over the phone was incredibly funny to me."

In a good year, Sam has made fifty thousand dollars as a female phone fantasy.

But Candi found phone sex a drag. A different piece of technology figured in her own fantasies. It's not the phone but the camera. "Nude modeling is the fulfillment of a fantasy for me. To be paid sixty to one hundred dollars an hour to lie around relaxed and be nude and have a guy with a camera adore me—that's fulfillment."

Candi lives modestly in an artists' complex where she is able to walk around naked most of the time. "The men," she says, "are very supportive of my nudity." (And who says all men are rats?) She earns a little money modeling and taking nude photos of men that they then use to answer swinger ads. The camera has no gender; it swings both ways.

She says she used to wish for "a rich, handsome, sweet, lovable boyfriend who would give me money, but now I want friends who'll do that."

"What friends will do that for you?" I ask. And for the first time in our conversation, Candi looks away and stares out the window for a long time. "I'm sorry," she says, "I fogged out."

She does have her dreams, her own sexual fantasies which, wild as they are, she gladly describes: "I like to imagine romance, to think of being taken out, of flirting —of a real relationship."

In an age of phone fantasies and camera caresses, that's the ultimate fetish.

six

LOVE

in the

TIME

of DIET

COLA

Whoever You Are, I Can't Get You Out of My Mind

What would happen if overcommitted, professional SWM actually found attractive, intelligent, spunky woman for serious but spontaneous relationship?

A hundred times a day in a hundred cities, a man and a woman lock eyes for a second and this question comes up. Then they walk on, faces in a crowd, and the feeling passes.

But what happened to—let's call him—"Jeff" is that the feeling didn't go away. He was in San Francisco on business, and there she was. "It was my frame of mind at the time," he recalled. "And you know how it is when you're traveling—you do things you wouldn't do in your hometown."

It wasn't so much what Jeff did that bothered him. It's what he didn't do.

A week after a chance encounter with a woman on a San Francisco street corner, he sat in his office in Boston and decided to place the following ad in *The San Francisco Chronicle:* "Woman frantically searching for taxi corner Market and Kearney, 5:45 P.M. We spoke too briefly. . . ."

This desperately seeking, frantically searching ad was buried among a series of thank-yous to Saint Jude and a request from a researcher for interviews with survivors of Hiroshima and Nagasaki. Not the usual Singles Bars Anonymous, where the discreet seek and meet.

When I phoned Jeff to ask about the ad, he said he had never done anything like that before. "I saw this woman walking down the street looking for something," he recalled. "And I said to myself: This woman is perfect." The all-too-briefly-spoken words that ignited this flame of long-distance longing were:

HE: What are you looking for?
SHE: A cab.

"If I'd been quicker on my feet, I'd have spoken more to her before I crossed the street," said Jeff. "But the East Coast is not as friendly as the West Coast. I've lived in big cities all my life, and walking back across the street seemed as if it would be too threatening to her. I began regretting it immediately."

Oddly enough, Jeff could not recall what the perfect woman looked like or what she was wearing. "What struck me is not something I can answer. She was poised and well dressed—conservatively dressed, like a businesswoman—and she had a look of self-reliance. She was perky, cute, spunky—spunky is the key word here."

He described the experience as a "subcerebral reaction." In another age, poets would have said that Jeff had been hit with one of Cupid's arrows. But your totally modern dude has learned to subconsciously extract the dart and ignore the bleeding.

"Had I been quicker, I could have saved money," said Jeff. The ad ran for a week and cost forty-seven dollars. Six days went by without a single response. Then on the seventh day, *she* stopped resting.

Shortly before your inquiring reporter called him, one woman responded to Jeff's ad. He's not sure if this one is The One, but she was on that corner around that time, and she was looking for a cab. She's going to send Jeff her picture.

Jeff says he's not a terribly impulsive person, but the incident reminded him of something his father once told him before he knew that fathers know best. "My dad said that timing is the most important thing in life," Jeff recalled. "I argued with my dad about absolutely everything, but he was right."

At forty, Jeff is still a bachelor, although he's not committed to staying that way. If the woman in the photo isn't the one, they'll probably have a drink sometime anyway. She's a stewardess and flies East regularly.

And . . . if she is the lady whose brief glance pierced his heart, what will he do? "Then," he says, "I'll be on the next plane to San Francisco."

All of this brings me to my question. If you were the handsome young man in the black coat on the uptown IRT in New York in the spring of 1965, and you sat across from a spunky young college girl who was me and mouthed the words, "I love you," why did you get off at Seventy-second Street?

Nothing but a WASP

All weekend long I've had this blues song in my head. It's a little tune that goes something like this:

> *Gimme a big WASP man.*
> *I mean a big WASP man.*
> *I'll make him meat loaf 'n' mashed potatoes,*
> *Every chance I can—*
> *I wanna big WASP man.*

You see, Doctor, it all began when I was talking to another woman at work about cute guys. Cute guys. *Homo cuticus.*

We are both mature, responsible, kinda now, kinda with-it women. We have held jobs, bought property and delivered babies. We have Significant Others whom we have no intention of leaving. But what our SOs don't know won't hurt them. So what we like to do is talk about cute guys.

That, Dr. Freud, is what women want to do.

In the course of our conversation, I mentioned this guy who I thought was cute, and she said, "But he's so WASP." (And what is Robert Redford—chopped liver?)

The implication was that by being a WASP, my dreamboat was immediately excluded from cute-guyness. That is the sad fact of male WASP life today. They rule corporate America. They can join the best private clubs. Advertisers cater to them. Caterers cater to them. But women are dismissing them. Somewhere on the road to power, the WASP lost his sex appeal.

This, of course, is poor Georgie Bush's problem. He's a WASP, and that has become translated as WIMP (White Impotent Male Pastry).

Now, maybe I'm just weird. Maybe I'm too much the sexual liberal. Maybe it's because it's spring. But I still like to cruise the Financial District and ogle the guys in wingtips. You simply never know what they've got in their portfolios.

And that is the charm of the WASP. In a dress-for-sex-success world, they've made no concessions. You will never see any jewelry beyond an occasional wedding band. No gold neck chains. No pinky rings. And, thank God—never an earring.

They are buttoned and tied right up to their freshly shaved chins. No stubble. No chest hair. No Calvin Klein's Obsession.

Only yours.

It's left to your female imagination to conjure up the male animal lurking beneath that pin-striped hide. In all his blandness, the WASP is your baby. You can do with him what you will.

And his civil tongue and civil exterior will never let on. He will never shake your hand and say, "Gee, it's swell to meet you, Mrs. Kahn. You go right ahead and have wild fantasies about me. I'll be at the club if you need me."

El WASP. He's out of fashion. He's got skin like Wonder bread. If you mentally undress him, you'd better have a suit hanger and shoehorns handy.

But his blandness is your tabula rasa, your blank slate

for writing a romance novel. Imagine him in his Burberry, carrying you in his big WASP arms toward a split-level in Connecticut.

Devil take the briefcase!

Women's Glib—
All About Al

Of course I was excited when Ellen told me she was getting married. I mean, how much longer could she stand to play the zany, uncommitted Molly Dodd? Wasn't it time for Ellen to throw in the Laura Ashley towel and join the hip housewives of "thirtysomething"?

"So who's the lucky guy?" I was about to ask her. Then I remembered Al. What woman could forget Al? It all began last summer in Manhattan when I had a conversation with Sonya Bourgeoise, the performance-anxiety artist.

Sonya had told me she'd been perfectly happy since leaving San Francisco. She said she had more work than she could handle. But when it came to Al, she sang a different song, and it went something like this: I left my dynamite orgasm in San Francisco.

"Al . . . Al was fantastic in bed but totally unambitious. . . ." she had told me as we sat around her loft eating Cajun chicken wings. "Now I'm dating Bernie, who's an editor at *Time*. Gorgeous. Brilliant. Perfect clothes. Plays handball with Donnie Trump. But he hasn't the slightest notion of what women want. Al knew. Sometimes I really miss Al."

"I'll bet you do," I said, licking my wing.

"So I hear Al is seeing Ellen Cusak," she said, dipping

her wing in the Louisiana hot sauce. "She's the one who designs the sets for the San Francisco Ballet."

"I think Ellen lost that job," I said.

"Well, her career may be in trouble, but I'll tell you this: Ellen is gettin' it good."

I suppose it's progress. One of the big changes I've noticed in women these past few years is how they now rate men on their performances. Didn't women once berate men for doing the same thing?

It's not just kiss and tell; it's kiss and critique.

Sonya went on to describe Al's boffo technique. He got nothing but raves:

"Al—You'll come out of the theater humming a song."

"Al— ★ ★ ★ ★ "

"Al—Siskel and Ebert say, 'Two thumbs ups.' "

And now, months after learning more than I'd ever want to know about Al, I sat there in the Zuni Cafe looking at Ellen, the woman who bagged him. At thirty-sevensomething, she was hardly the blushing fiancée. I *had* to ask.

"Ellen, the guy you're marrying—is he that one you were seeing who used to see Sonya Bourgeoise—the guy who . . ."

"Al," she said. "I'm marrying Al."

Well, this was news. I could hardly contain myself. How do you say in English: Congratulations on landing the greatest stud on earth?

"Ellen, I'm overjoyed for you. . . ." I said in all sincerity.

Just then the waiter at the Zuni came to take our order.

"What's a mesclum of lettuce?" Ellen asked.

"A mesclum? Well, that's just a mixture. . . ." he said.

"And what are garlic chapons?" Ellen asked.

What would she ask next: Are your chapons as good as Al's chapons?

"Say, what's a salad landaise?" I asked.

The waiter was getting impatient. I expected him to say, "Landaise is French for what's-it-to-you, *merde*-head."

When we had gotten through the ordeal and the vocabulary of lunch, I tried to steer the conversation back to Al the Greatest.

"So Al . . ." I said. "Al is . . ."

"Unemployed," Ellen quickly offered.

"And what is it Al doesn't do for a living?" I asked.

"Fine carpentry," she said.

OK. I had to let her know that I knew all about Al and his magic hammer. So I told her the whole story. Sonya. Chicken wings. I didn't spare a detail.

Ellen just laughed the laugh of the well-satisfied. She said she'd have to tell Al what I knew about what he knows about What Women Want.

So now I'm looking forward to the day when I finally meet Al at a party. He'll be standing there leaning against a pine china cabinet—six feet three, tight Levi's, a plaid flannel shirt over a light blue T-shirt, reddish hair and beard, green eyes, the faint smell of Watco emanating from his long, slender fingers.

"So you're Al," I'll say, seeing stars . . . four stars.

"Yeah," he'll say. "I'm Al. *That* Al."

Then I'll pause and say, "Do you do floors?"

I Gave My Love a Lawn Mower...

There are two kinds of people you cannot buy presents for. One is men; the other is husbands. If your husband is a man, the situation is utterly impossible.

Even if you buy something seemingly innocuous like a shirt, you come up against men and their weird tailoring cults. Things that mean nothing to a normal person carry all sorts of significance for men.

There's a secret code in things like shirt collars—not unlike the meanings youth gangs attach to tattoos. For instance, I once bought my husband a shirt at Macy's that said nothing special to me, but to him the collar was like a neon sign saying: "Gay and Cruising."

The life cycle of the average man can be divided into three phases: the button-down years (BD), the anti-button-down years (AD), and the AB/BD era. Failure to read the signs can result in domestic sartorial violence.

Selecting other simple items, like ties, is also out. Giving a tie is the equivalent of collaborating with the oppressor.

Make no mistake—the issue is manliness. Anything chosen by a woman is potentially sissy.

Finally, one is left with thoughts like: Well, goddammit, then I'm going to give him something *I* want him to have. That's when I decided on the perfect gift—a lawn mower.

Before buying my husband the power mower, I attempted to gain the complicity of his best friend. The friend refused to desert the fraternity. Even in an era of power ties and power lunches, a power mower could be viewed as unmanly, the brother said. Real men do things the hard way.

So I made up my mind. I was going to buy him a weed whip. No questions asked.

I went to Pastime Hardware, a store where they sell nails and drills and chain saws. There were men in the store in cowboy hats looking at manure spreaders. There's a gun shop across the street. How could I go wrong?

The clerk—himself a man—showed me the deluxe weed whip, then volunteered, "But you know you're paying a lot for the Black and Decker name. You could probably find a cheaper one at a discount place."

I drove across town to Payless, where I was delighted to find they had weed whips on sale. I made it as far as the checkout line when a clerk—undeniably male—stopped me. "Let me see that," he said, snatching the weed whip from the jaws of victory.

He fiddled with the starter switch. "I don't like this at all. I wouldn't buy it," he said generously. All I wanted was an end to present-shopping. The honest clerk continued. "Listen, there's a good hardware store called Pastime where you could probably find a Black and Decker."

Are these guys in cahoots?

I ended up buying my husband a Samsonite garment bag. He opened it and said, "Now why do I need this?" and I brought it back the next day.

But there was one other little present he loved. It was a piece of wooden kitsch that I found at a variety store's going-out-of-business sale. I'm not sure if he loved the gift that much or he just liked the fifty-cent price tag I left on to please him.

It was a wall plaque called Wifey's Mood Barometer. It included a wheel with a dial that could be set to sweet (drawing of sugar), sour (lemon), stubborn (mule), bossy (rolling pin), silly (goose), etc.

I keep setting it to sweet, but someone keeps turning the needle to dangerous (knives).

It's a problem to set because there are only eight choices, and a woman's day takes her through many subtle gradations. There are days when I can go from laid-back (willow leaf) to PMS (weed whip) in seconds.

The hubbyometer, however, required only one setting: impossible.

What Makes Seth Cool?

Sometimes you meet a guy who's, like, so terrific and stuff that you want to know more about him. Seth Altshuler is that kind of guy.

Mainly, I see Seth at the school bus stop when I walk my daughter Hannah there on her way to the fourth grade. Seth is a fifth-grader. With his reddish hair, blue eyes and freckles, he could probably replace Fred Savage on "The Wonder Years." And he's the world's foremost authority.

He can tell you which dogs in the neighborhood are on the loose. And which girls are wild. Ask him about a certain junior high girl and he will say, "Oh, you hear all kinds of rumors about her."

"What kind of rumors?" one asks immediately.

"Oh, ya know, she's going with this one or she's going with that one," he says wearily.

I wanted to know more about Seth. What makes him tick? What are his hopes and dreams? What does he know and when did he know it?

The interview took place as we did lunch at Edy's Ice Cream Parlor, Seth's favorite restaurant. I was accompanied by Hannah, who acted as a co-interviewer and watchdog to make sure her mother did not act too embarrassing.

Hannah had a tuna sandwich and a hot caramel sundae with extra whipped cream. Seth selected the BLT of the day and a chocolate sundae with extra whipped cream. When the waitress brought my shrimp salad, Seth said approvingly, "My dad loves that stuff."

I got right to the point and asked Seth how he dealt with the violent, crazy world he lives in. He talked about the gangs in school and in the movies. "Some people have heard of the Crips or H_2O or the Bloods," he said. "I've never had anyone come up to me and pull a knife. But someone who just thinks they're tough? Usually you can outwit them." As he said "outwit," he pointed to his head.

"Like how?" I asked.

"I'll say a word they have no idea the meaning of."

"A big word?"

"Not exactly, but something that sounds *sophisticated*. Like that word. That's the way I get out of it."

Hannah jumped right into the interview game, trying to get at Seth's essence. "How do you think you act?" she asked. "Like, do you act wild or normal?"

"At a party with parents, you act gentle," he said. Then he smiled slyly and added: "But on the playground, I'm *wild*. No question about it."

We talked about favorite subjects, and both Hannah and Seth said they loved math. To Seth, history seemed irrelevant. "History is things in the past . . . the sixties . . . color TV, but math seems to tie in to more things."

I asked him how he saw math helping in his stated desire to be (1) a soccer player, (2) an actor, (3) maybe a comedian.

"Well, math skills wouldn't affect my job, but in terms of my life, math has the biggest effect. Like, this isn't a full glass," he said pointing to his Coke. "It's three-fourths full. That's math."

I asked him what he would put in a time capsule for

the future. We talked about fluorescent-green surfer shorts, Town & Country T-shirts, a New Edition record. . . .

"I'd put in a whole bunch of hair supplies, like gel," said Hannah.

This led to a discussion of status symbols, and Seth brought up his "stripes"—three horizontal lines cut into his hair on both sides above the ears. He said he took a lot of teasing for this haircut. "Mainly black people have these. So someone on the bus said, 'What are you, black or white? Like, make up your mind.' They were actually getting kind of racist. I know it's a big statement, but I don't consider a haircut *black*. Like, some people say, 'Don't wear that shirt, it's a girl's.' I don't consider a shirt a *girl's* . . ."

Hannah interrupted, "What about a skirt?"

Seth stopped his speech and said, "Well . . . yeah."

Seth is quick, but he's also thoughtful. I wanted to know where his confidence came from. What did his parents do right?

"My parents are the life of everything I do," he said. "They just give me a start, and then I put it together. I got the gentle side from my mom. But my dad was *exactly* like me when he was a kid." He says it as if he were there. As if he could imagine his father's childhood.

"He got into trouble usually, and he was good at sports. We have the same characteristics. I feel sad for kids who are left alone. I think if you know your parents, you know yourself."

"Well, what's the worst thing parents can do?" I asked.

Seth homed in on hypocrisy, "Saying things like, 'Hey, son, let's talk about Just Say No. And while you're up—get me a Coors.' "

Moving on to another subject, I said in my best Barbara Walters manner, "Seth, you've had five girlfriends since the fourth grade. What's the secret of your way with women?"

Hannah looked me dead in the eye and interjected, "The worst thing parents can do is embarrass their kids."

Seth the charmer, the lady-killer, came right to my rescue: "But that's their job."

My Life as a Man

I can't make it in this man's world. Life would be so much easier if I had a wife. Life would be so much easier if I were a man.

What modern woman hasn't had these thoughts? Those of us struggling to lift ourselves up by our bra straps often feel the deck is stacked against us. Men don't have to "prove" anything. Men can do an OK job; women have to be great. Men were taught from childhood to be aggressive; we were taught to be nice. Men are encouraged to go for it; we are encouraged to lose weight.

In an attempt to understand what the world looks like to someone who has all these advantages, I decided to be Man for a Day. What would happen, I wondered, if I walked a mile in his big leather shoes? A bit of makeup, a few new items of clothing, a different haircut and— *voilà*—little Alice became Big Al.

The first thing I noticed was the frightened look on my husband's face when he woke up and saw me standing there dousing myself with Stud, the aftershave for men who want to make a stink.

I was about to say, "You get those buns out of bed and make me some breakfast" when I realized that I hadn't made him breakfast since our fifth anniversary. Sure, for a few years I cooked, cleaned and was his all-around love slave. But after a while it was every person for itself.

Later, one of the kids took a look at me in my baggy pleated pants, felt hat, suspenders and tie and said, "Mom, don't try to be cool. Maybe Diane Keaton can get away with that, but it just isn't you."

As soon as they were all out of the house, instead of my usual routine of not cleaning up and not doing the laundry, I put on my mustache and went out.

As I walked down the street I heard a man who passed me say, "Who was that? Madonna?"

"You've been listening to Joan Rivers," said his companion. "That was Wayne Newton."

I could pass.

At the office, I introduced myself to the guys as Big Al, the new guy.

"Hey, Big Al the New Guy," one of the fellas said, "want to go deer hunting with us after work? We're gonna kill for a couple of hours, then pick up some babes and party."

"Sorry," I said. "Can't make it."

"Whatsa matter, Al—you a sissy-boy?"

As if that weren't enough, the boss called me in at nine-fifteen. "Scotch, Al?" he said, offering me the bottle from the brown paper bag on his desk.

I declined. "Whatsa matter, Al—can't handle it?"

At lunchtime, I went to my favorite bar and grill. Instead of getting the Dieter's Delite, I told the waitress: "Give me the biggest, bloodiest, rawest hunk of meat you've got, a plate of fries, double cole slaw and some chocolate whipped-cream pie."

"No wonder you're so thin," she said. "You eat like a bird."

After lunch I walked over to the bookstore, hoping to find something hard-boiled to carry around but not actually read.

"Where's the Men's section?" I asked the clerk.

"We have no Men's section," she answered.

"But that's not fair," I said indignantly. "You have a Women's section."

"Look, pal," she said to me, her voice dripping with sarcasm, "we consider the rest of the store the Men's section."

Back at work, I noticed Marge, the gofer, staring at me. I stared back at her. I was certain she'd guessed my identity.

"Marge, guess what's under here?" I said, smiling at her.

She stood up on her desk and started screaming, "Eek, a pervert!"

My sexual-harassment hearing is scheduled for next week.

When the boss heard about the charges, he offered me a raise. And the guys are taking me out to dinner. Phyllis, a gal in the secretarial pool, winked at me and said she would testify in my behalf. Then she asked if I would take her to the annual spring dance.

I think I'll wear a tux.

The Unimportance of Being Ken

In his twenty-nine years of existence, no one has ever devoted an entire story to the life of Ken. We aim to put an end to that. We hope to teach you things about Ken that will make you gasp and shout, "No! Not Ken." We hope to prove beyond a reasonable doubt that Ken represents the American male's worst nightmare—a guy who is little more than an accessory to some doll.

After an extensive investigation into Ken's background and a detailed interview with Ken's publicist, Candace Irving of Mattel Inc., we think we know what lurks beneath that hard plastic hollow torso marked "Ken © 1960."

Let's set the record straight: Ken is not gay. Rumors about Ken's sexual orientation surfaced several years ago when a Bob doll appeared on the scene. Bob is an anatomically correct Ken-like doll who came out of the closet several years ago.

Bob, however, is not to be perceived as Ken's little friend. In fact, "Bob is not even made by Mattel," says Ken's publicist. "Bob is a different market than Ken," she says unequivocally. "Bob is for adults."

Ken's very lack of anatomical anything makes it questionable whether he is even straight. But one thing is certain: Ken may correctly be perceived as a total wimp.

Ken exists for no other reason than to serve Barbie. When asked how she imagines Ken spending his day,

Irving said, "Oh, I think he is mowing Barbie's yard or checking on Barbie's pool or working as Barbie's handyman." She's a benevolent dominatrix, that Barbie.

"Doesn't this get a bit oppressive?" I questioned, trying—as we investigative reporters try—to put words in someone's mouth. I was hoping to get her to admit that Ken's life is hell, but Irving is a PR pro. "Well," she said, "he is going out with the world's most famous woman."

On the surface, it may appear that Ken has it made in the toy shade. Most little girls have several Barbies in the harem for Ken. In fact, sales are two Barbies to every Ken. But not every theme Barbie comes with a theme Ken. For example, last year when Magic Moves Barbie ran her fingers through her luxurious long blond hair, there was no Magic Moves Ken beside her. That's because last year's Ken had a molded head.

When Dreamtime Barbie appeared in her nightie, there was no Dreamtime Ken. "We wouldn't get that close to having them in nightclothes at the same time," explains Irving.

Compared with any other doll in the Barbie matriarchy, Ken has barely evolved from his original introduction as Barbie's boyfriend. Even Allen, who disappeared in the late sixties, and Curtis, the black doll, had independent existences. But for every Malibu Barbie there's a Malibu Ken. For every Walk Lively Barbie, there's a Walk Lively Ken. For every Busy Barbie, there's a Busy Ken—rendering him little more than tit for Barbie's tat.

Ken fashions have occasionally hinted at an independent existence for the 11¾-inch hunk. Over the years, we have seen outfits for Dr. Ken, American Airlines Captain Ken, Foundation Boy Ken, Mr. Astronaut Ken, Rovin' Reporter Ken, Business Appointment Ken—and even a turned-on, tuned-in Guruvy Ken in 1969.

That was also the fateful year a Talking Ken made his

appearance. (A Spanish Talking Ken followed pronto.) It was Talking Ken himself who undercut any suggestion that Ken actually worked for a living.

What did Ken say that year he broke silence? Because this rare interview is of such historic significance, I print the entire text here:

ME: Why do you let Barbie dominate you?
TALKING KEN: Barbie's a great dancer.
ME: What do you actually do?
T.K.: I'll get the food for the party.
ME: Are you avoiding my questions?
T.K.: Have you met Barbie's new friend?
ME: Come on, Ken, are you a man or a mouse?
T.K.: I'm taking the girls shopping . . . wanna go?
ME: Ken, are you into B&D?
T.K.: Put on some records and let's dance.
ME: Ken, isn't your posture as a party animal just a cover for alienation and ennui?
T.K.: PJ's having a party. Let's go.

It was hopeless. The more you pulled his string, the more you kept getting the same nonsense, as if he were some defeated prisoner of war, some Stepford husband. It was, sadly, the only time he ever spoke.

The real Ken, Ken Handler (whose father owned Mattel and named the original dolls after daughter Barbie and son Ken), does not grant interviews. "Don't even try to find him," cautions Irving. (I make a mental note to phone my literary agent and have her start pitching my new book proposal, *My Search for the Real Ken*.)

Irving is upbeat about Ken's future. "He will have a completely different look this year," she says. "More GQ-looking. His features will be more sculpted and . . ."

(here Irving drops the bomb) "the new Ken will have rooted hair!"

Not since the mid-seventies, when Mod Hair Ken had rooted hair down to his shoulders and New Look Ken came with decal beard, sideburns and two mustaches, has Ken's head been topped with anything other than molded plastic.

An anxious nation watches for this hairy hero. Will he, Samson-like, put on more power with his locks? Will the new Ken be more macho to compete with such rivals as GI Joe?

Alas for Ken, his market position demands eternal wimpiness. "GI Joe is a boy's toy," explains Irving. (No offense to Madonna.) "Boys view Ken as being a girl's toy exclusively. Although they may play with him at a girl's house, they wouldn't want the stigma of having their friends know."

Even as a playmate, Ken's in the closet.

Mattel, Irving assures me, does make toys for boys. In addition to Big Jim, Muscle and Master of the Universe, says Irving, "We're introducing a new collectible figure called Guts."

So as feminists snicker and empowered men beat the drum for his absent maleness, Ken stares blankly into toy purgatory. And, you know, the guy's only doing it for some doll.

Time After Time...
A Table for Two

Sam's Grill. White linen tablecloths. Dark wooden walls. Waiters in black tuxedos. A man at the bar wearing an ascot and sipping a martini.

It looks the way the world did when we first opened our eyes in the 1940s, which is how long Sam's Grill has been on Bush Street. It could be Tony's and it could be the Cafe Royal. The fundamental things survive.

I look at you across the table and think of our first date. I wore my new blue straight skirt and matching vest, with the button-down-collar blouse. Other kids at the party were doing the stroll, and you were talking to me about Nietzsche and George Bernard Shaw.

I was hoping you'd ask me to the senior prom. I was wondering if you were going to kiss me goodnight. When you did, I decided right then: Let's get married.

The waiter brings our dinner. Crusty bread, grilled fish, *au gratin* potatoes. A man and a woman having dinner.

I think of the summer after we graduated from high school. I worked in an office filing orders. You were a mailman. The night before we left for college, we went to Tony's. Chianti bottles. Checkered tablecloths. A glass filled with breadsticks. On the way home, in your father's Olds Holiday, we sang along with "Moon River" on the radio as we set off to see the world together.

We broke up three months later.

Tonight, we look around Sam's and see all the old people and talk of how our fathers would have liked it. I've told you about the time when I was five years old and my father stood up in the Cafe Royal and sang "O Sole Mio." Everyone clapped and said he sang just like Caruso. I remember this better than I remember his funeral. But I remember your father's funeral as if it were yesterday. A sunny day in San Diego, and our baby took her first steps without holding on. And we clapped. Then we went in and bowed our heads.

Our baby is fourteen now, and you wonder if she would like Sam's. "It wouldn't mean anything to her," you say.

"What would she order?" I say. "There's nothing here she likes."

Clam chowder. Fresh asparagus. Grilled Pacific snapper. There are no new words on the menu. We have no questions for the waiter.

Remember a poem we loved in college about a time made simple by the loss of detail?

The summer after we graduated from college, we decided we were going to get married. You told me I would learn to cook and drive and balance a checkbook. Two out of three ain't bad.

I worked at Kroch's and Brentano's selling children's books. You drove a cab in Evanston. We ate our last Chicago pizza and planned our voyage to California. When we arrived, all we heard was Bob Dylan singing "Like a Rolling Stone." We were on our own.

We got married a year later.

That was half our life ago. Whenever we go out to dinner—just the two of us—I think of us at nineteen, posing as grown-ups. Drinking manhattans in Manhattan and then falling asleep during *Goldfinger*. Eating lobster for the first time at the Miss Florence Diner in Florence, Massachusetts. Fighting in Paris in 1967, a big public fight in a cafe. What was it about? We both got up and went our separate ways. We could have lost each other there in the sixth arrondissement.

There are no fajitas at Sam's Grill. Or arugula. Nothing Cajun. The coat hooks are solid brass. The booths are dim and private. The waiter brings everything promptly. When the check comes, we're in no hurry to leave and find the eighties waiting at the door.

What sights we've seen since that party in high school when we left early to talk about serious stuff. But it's the same old story. As we walk out of Sam's Grill, I marvel at my luck. I'm still leaving with the most interesting guy at the party.

seven

The

MOMENT

When

HISTORY

BEGAN

These Are a Few of My
Favorite Years

NEW YEAR'S EVE 1951: I vow to stay up until midnight.
My mother and I go shopping and buy blue metallic top
hats that say 1951 in silver glitter.

We buy pink Hawaiian leis and noisemakers. We get
a lazy Susan tray from the deli with corned beef, pas-
trami and tongue. I learn what tongue is; I nearly die.

That night I wear my pink angora sweater and my
gray felt skirt and my patent-leather Mary Janes. At eight
o'clock my mother puts out the food. I hear the man on
the radio dedicate a new song to our boys in Korea. It's
"Till Then (When All The World Will Be Free)."

I eat everything on the bottom tier of the lazy Susan
except the tongue. I get very, very sick and am put to
bed at ten o'clock.

NEW YEAR'S EVE 1960: I go out on my first New
Year's Eve date. I am sixteen and hot stuff. Three boys
have asked me out, and I go with Mike Levin, a senior,
whom I have a crush on from Student Council.

I wear a black jersey sheath with a white Peter Pan
collar, size seven, and black spike heels with pointy toes.
We go to party at a motel (!) where there are college boys
(!) and liquor! I drink a screwdriver. I dance with a
strange boy who asks for my phone number and calls me
at eight the next morning.

Someone puts Mathis on the hi-fi. People start making out passionately, wantonly, in front of everyone. I nearly die. I try not to look. At midnight, everybody starts kissing everybody. Wait until I tell my girlfriend Penny.

Mike Levin takes me outside where it is 20 degrees and kisses me so sweetly I'm sure I'm in love. Two weeks later, I start going steady with another boy.

NEW YEAR'S EVE 1963: I live in New York and go to college. I still tease my hair because the First Lady does. I wear a maroon A-line sleeveless dress with a matching jacket and square-toed, short-heeled shoes.

My date takes me to see *Waiting for Godot* at a small theater. Afterward, we go to a party. People are talking softly and drinking scotch and soda and smoking Camels and Gauloises. Miles is on the stereo playing "Kind of Blue."

Round about midnight, people outside are shooting guns. Someone could die. Or they couldn't. We keep talking about Nietzsche and Camus and Being and Nothingness.

NEW YEAR'S EVE 1971: All Power to the People. We are in Berkeley at a house on Berkeley Way. I'm wearing my Mary Tyler Moore bell-bottoms and my surplus-store black turtleneck and hiking boots and some lucky beads I have strung myself. You never know when it'll all come down and we'll have to retreat to the mountains.

Some are on mushrooms and some are on mescaline and some have gotten clearlight tabs from the Dolores Street Supermarket. Some do reefer and others just sip from the bottle of mescal with a worm in it. Some do everything.

I'm having a good time, but I know that people are

dying in Vietnam. Around ten, the session begins. We've got horns, guitar, drums, piano and weird little things holy Tibetans play.

At midnight we kiss, but we never stop playing. Men kiss each other. Someone grabs my rear end. Watch it, pig!

By 2:00 A.M. I'm playing the piano with my knuckles. We sound great. The little kids are thinking: As soon as I'm old enough, I'm voting for Reagan.

NEW YEAR'S EVE 1980: I vow to stay up until midnight, but the party starts at nine and by then I'm ready to go to bed. My baby is nine months old, and she still doesn't sleep through the night. I'm wearing something that makes it easy to nurse her. Maybe if I drink some champagne it'll make her sleepy too.

We eat a feast of red pepper shrimp, tortellini with pesto, bouillabaisse, Cuban bread and Boursin cheese. Jayme has brought her homemade cannoli.

At midnight, I kiss my family. I kiss the old acquaintances who'll never be forgot. We gather around the piano and sing "Is That All There Is?"

The Alumni News: Class Notes

CLASS OF 1915: Sadly, the only news I have is the passing of Chauncy Portman. Portie took his traditional evening brandy and passed away in Summerville, Maine. For more on our class, see "In Memory." Anyone else out there with good news, please write.

CLASS OF 1926: Thorp Jenkins is doing well after a hip replacement. He writes to say that his book of poetry, *The Flame at Twilight*, is ready for publication. Here is a sample:

THE ROAD TAKEN

Another two roads, another two woods,
I took one—
So much for shoulds.
I knew you, you knew me,
Time has gone,
Where have we been?
I took the road everyone did,
What of it—
Life shuts the lid.

CLASS OF 1937: Earl Salomen ran into Tut Malone on the beach at Naples, Fla. Earl says Tut wanted to play tennis even though he is recovering from a hernia repair.

Those of you who were at the fiftieth reunion will remember the way Tut performed on the basketball court before he was carried off. . . . We also heard from Bob Phalen, who is completing his book, *A Grand Piano from Scratch in Your Workshop*. . . . Chauncy Portman, Jr., and his loyal wife Betsy (the fair Betsy Goodnough, Vassar '40) have returned from a cruise in time to see their first great-grandchild on their way home to Newport.

CLASS OF 1946: Bump Hampton and Cap Drebble have had a contest to see who can lose the most weight. Bump's on the Cape Cod lobster diet and Cap's on the Sarasota ice-cream diet. . . . Tom Nielsen and his Dianna report that retirement from the military allows them more time to see their ten grandchildren and three Dalmatians and to finish *The Guns and Butter Cookbook*. . . . Trip Thalmeyer says that this is really it. After divorces from Laura Layton (Holyoke '48) and Dorothy Singleton (Stanford '53), the Tripper has a new lady, Kiki Ralston (Cal State Dominguez Hills '79) and is recovering nicely from the triple bypass.

CLASS OF 1959: Chauncy Portman III reports that daughter Erin will be entering the class of '92 this fall. Chaunce, who has just been named CEO of Standard Pharmaceuticals, says he can "just about afford it." . . . Silt Wilson ran into Stansfield Broom, who is now Sister Marlene, an Episcopal nun. . . . Dump Cook has been named head of the new Medieval Sciences Department at the college and has published *Where We Stand: A Look Back*. This must be reading for all alums.

CLASS OF 1968: Matt Mowry, now called Rama Dam, writes that the ashram is always open to his old classmates. . . . Tyler Wilson, recently appointed urban affairs director by President Reagan, says he bears no ill

will for his old campus nickname, "the black guy." . . .
Kent Goldstein writes from L.A., where he is producing
a TV series based on his experiences as a computer programmer in Nam. . . . New parents Sylvia and Kip
Hampton report that the twins, Jimi and Janis, are doing
well.

CLASS OF 1983: Holly Mooney-Schwemmer is doing
an internship at Albert Einstein in Psychogynecology.
. . . Seth Cleary has left Charles Schwab for Prudential-
Bache. . . . Nicole Dawson has married Lawrence Law-
son (Smith '82). The Dawson-Lawsons will start Columbia Law School this fall. . . . Buzz Baskin thanks the
class of '91 for hosting Gay and Lesbian Alumni Weekend. . . . Chip Stevens writes that he just started on his
M.B.A. at Berkeley and that he still wears shoes and
believes in capitalism. . . . Bring your beanies to the
fifth this summer!

Joe Variable Rate, Meet Mary Fixed

When I started going out to big parties in college, you began a conversation with, "What's your major?" That was the way you categorized people. Oh, she's a social-science type—probably plays the guitar and cares about cats and people. Or, he's a lit twit—probably eats madeleines and smokes a pipe. Or, he's studying engineering—actually needs to earn a living.

Sometime after high school, I think we all become aware that there is some kind of class system out there. But we also sensed that "petit bourgeois" and "lumpen proletariat" didn't quite describe America.

After college and whatever graduate education we used to put off growing up, the party question became "What do you do?" Oh, an options trader—how interesting. (Yuppie scum.) Oh, a tenants' rights lawyer—how wonderful. (All that education for a lousy 35K.) Oh, an artist. (What does your daddy do?)

But today all these inquiries seem irrelevant. You aren't what you majored in. You aren't what you do. And contrary to recent theories about the importance of zip codes in identifying socioeconomic groups, I don't think you are where you live. Not exactly. It's how and when you got there. You are your real estate situation.

It's more subtle than renters vs. homeowners, although this is the obvious major distinction.

262 – Alice Kahn

Recently I had dinner with Bud and Kitten (not their real names), two apparently successful baby boomers. They had just moved to Los Angeles from New York. They sold their beautiful house on Long Island Sound for 450K and were now looking for something comparable on the West Coast. It turns out that a fixer-upper, three-bedroom home in any neighborhood they would consider—one with amenities such as Uzi-free nights and fewer smog-alert days—begins in the 700K ballpark. Their timing was wrong. Their direction was wrong. They were forced into downward mobility.

It occurred to me that the party question should be "Are you in the real estate market now, were you in the market five years ago, or are you shut out?" But the groups are even further distinguished by how the deal was done.

My friend Cinderella views herself as one of the Real Estateless. She's in her thirties and a successful writer. She has a deal with Spielberg. She's got a handsome boyfriend. She's naturally thin. She lives in what the zip code demographers call a "Money and Brains" neighborhood. But she's a renter. Although she appears to have it all, timing shut Cindy out of the real estate market. "I'll never be able to buy a home, and I hate everybody who has one," she says.

Her hate isn't doled out equally. The people whom Cindy hates most are the people who buy with RR financing—that's rich relatives making the down payment. Cindy's own folks need every 40K they've got, and her boyfriend's parents don't even have that.

Cindy says she has some respect for another group— the Self-Mades. These are people who have actually purchased homes with money they *earned*. (Money made from selling drugs does not count. Drugs are like rich relatives—addicting and debilitating.)

The Self-Mades don't have to be at the mercy of their landlords or their rich relatives. Instead, they're at the mercy of their mortgages, which tends to make them politically conservative. They did it. The system works. So what's everyone else's problem?

The problem for many RRs is guilt, from whence all liberalism flows. They are plagued by their good fortune. But RR minus guilt equals conservatism. I got mine— call your own daddy.

The Real Estateless are either apathetic pessimists or coffeehouse radicals. They want the rules changed or they won't play your Monopoly game. They want to see rent control on Park Place and low-income housing on Marvin Gardens.

Conservative RRs and Self-Mades vote their square footage. How did baby boomers help elect corny old George Bush? It's just that longing for home . . . ownership.

While they strongly support a clean environment, a lasting peace and reproductive choice, they want to do it from their own 3 BR, 2 + BA.

The Moment When History Began

I was sitting in the New Asia Cafe on Broadway and 114th having lunch with Mike Segal. He had just asked me if I was a virgin, when the music on the radio stopped. "We interrupt this program to report that President Kennedy has just been shot in Dallas. . . ."

Where were you?

Mike Segal was wearing a gray tweed jacket and a blue plaid scarf. At first we ignored the announcement and kept eating egg foo yung and drinking jasmine tea. I was sure I hadn't heard it right.

"Wait a minute," I said, as Mike Segal attempted to get personal again. "Did he say someone had been shot?"

"Maybe it has something to do with Madame Nhu's visit," he said.

Then he explained that someone named Madame Nhu from a country I had never heard of called Vietnam had spoken at Columbia University that day. He had protested her visit.

Mike Segal was "political." I had never met anyone like him before. To think you know what's right for your government at the age of nineteen—not to support everything the president did—was unimaginable to me.

But I didn't say these things to Mike Segal, because I had only been in Manhattan for three months and this was only our fourth date. I coyly tried to conceal the truth. I was the worst thing you could be in sophisticated New York: I was a hick from the Midwest.

Still, a hick from Chicago is not totally innocent. I knew about local politics. Local politics were simple cash transactions. Fixed tickets. Calls to ward committeemen. The fiefdom of Richard J. Daley was a straightforward place.

But Washington was a complicated place. Washington was part of history. I didn't pay much attention to it until that day when the announcer said, "I repeat: The president has been shot. He is said to be moribund. . . ."

Moribund? Did that mean bound for death or still alive?

The know-it-all look left Mike Segal's face. We put down our forks. He left some money for the check. The date was over. We wandered out into the street and said good-bye in a daze.

I walked over to Juilliard to find my friend who was in dance class. By the time I got there, the meaning of moribund was clear. Girls in black leotards were leaning against the mirror sobbing as they stood in weird Martha Graham poses.

For the rest of the week, everyone walked up and down Broadway, learning history from newspapers and TV sets in shopwindows.

Since that day, I've carried around this box of old newspapers from one coast to the other like some people carry a favorite teddy bear from childhood. The *New York Post*, Friday, November 22, 1963: the entire front page is only a headline—JFK SHOT TO DEATH. *The New York Times*, Saturday, November 23: KENNEDY IS KILLED BY SNIPER AS HE RIDES IN CAR IN DALLAS; JOHNSON SWORN IN ON PLANE. *The New York Times*, Monday, November 25: PRESIDENT'S ASSASSIN SHOT TO DEATH IN JAIL CORRIDOR BY A DALLAS CITI-

ZEN; GRIEVING THRONGS VIEW KENNEDY BIER. Then, the *New York Daily News*, Monday, September 28, 1964: OSWALD ALONE THE KILLER.

That last headline was the beginning of an intense questioning of everything the government said and did. We all became political. Whatever security lay in not asking why was over.

For a year, we've been having anniversaries of the events of the late sixties. Twenty years since Sergeant Pepper. Twenty years since RFK was shot. Twenty years since Martin Luther King, Jr.'s death. Twenty years since Soviet tanks rolled into Prague. Twenty years since "the kids" got gassed at the Democratic convention in Chicago. Twenty years since a generation dropped acid.

But it all began on November 22, 1963. "Where were you when Kennedy died?" became a conversational cliché among my generation. So I clutch my pile of old newspapers now and remember how I felt in the New Asia Cafe then.

The news saved me from having to answer Mike Segal's question. When we said good-bye forever on Broadway I think we both knew. Nobody was a virgin anymore.

These Foolish Things
Remind Me of You

Penny is gone, and I can't think of anything else. Penny, my best friend, dead in Plano, Texas, in her forties.

She was my friend in high school, but we drifted apart. I think I've seen her twice in twenty years. So why do I feel as if I've just lost my best friend?

Our paths kept almost crossing, but we rarely managed to be in the same state at the same time. The last time I saw her was ten years ago in front of the merry-go-round on the beach boardwalk at Santa Cruz. We both had little girls and walked all over town pushing our umbrella strollers and catching up. She was traveling in California, and the meeting gave me a chance to learn her strange story.

I had left the hometown, Chicago, before she did and moved to New York. The year I left New York, Penny moved there. She was employed as a social worker and studied acting. She met a guy named Shelly, an adman, and they got married. Following a spiritual leader with the unlikely name of Lester, they moved to Sedona, Arizona.

Later, Penny became a born-again Christian, finally a "charismatic Catholic." She said to me, "You know me . . . I'll always be a charismatic something." She and her husband, who changed his name to John, became the caretakers at an unusual Catholic church built into the beautiful red rocks of mountainous Sedona.

Did I mention that when I knew her she was your proverbial "nice Jewish girl"?

When we met in California, her conversation was peppered with phrases she repeated like slogans—"Praise the Lord" and "What a blessing." For weeks afterward, every time I saw a pretty flower, a little voice would go off in my head, "What a blessing!"

I thought Penny was a saint. Not because she spent her adolescent summers working at a camp for severely handicapped people. Not because she left college to work with Chicago's toughest street gangs. But because she once refused to go to a popular girl's pajama party because I wasn't invited. She told me my corny poems were wonderful. She sat up with me playing her brother's Frank Sinatra album, *Only the Lonely*, after Tommy and I broke up.

Six weeks ago she called me after seeing my column in the Plano paper. I hadn't heard from her in at least eight years. She told me she had four children, ages twelve, ten, eight and six. She and her husband ran a drug-treatment program for teenagers in Plano. Just that week I had seen a survey listing her town as one of the safest places in America and mine as one of the most dangerous.

The conversation was fairly mundane until I asked how she was doing. "I'm kind of walking in a miracle now," she said. "In May I was told I had cancer."

She told me how she prayed and believed she was getting better. That her hair had fallen out from the radiation therapy. That she could put up with anything as long as it was temporary. That her doctor didn't understand why she prayed. That she had never been separated from her children.

Last week her husband called and said she was gone. I just can't believe it. Penny not in this world? Penny, whom I tried to make smile with her braces on. Penny, who tinted her hair honey blond and became a knockout at sixteen. Penny, who taught me how to do the twist.

I got out the old yearbook and said good-bye to her picture. I read what she wrote: ". . . Alice, since that day that I found out that you knew the words to 'Daddy Cool' I've admired you. It's funny that a song like that could start such a wonderful friendship. The summer when we began our diets and lost all that weight, our trip to Wisconsin to see your sister, all our wonderful times that I'll never forget—Our midnight talks, those were the times we really let our hair down . . . I can only hope (sorry to repeat the same words again) that no matter what the future holds for us I can always say that Alice Nelson is my friend. As long as I can say that I know I will not be lost or insecure. May God bless you and grant your every wish. Please Alice, always stay as wonderful as you are now, for no one could ever ask for more in a friend. Love always, Penny."

You see what I lost. No one will ever talk like that to me again. Oh, reader, if you ever had a best friend, call her today.

Are We in California Yet, Mommy?

Moving. Don't expect me to talk about anything else for a while. Moving. Leaving the block where I've lived for twenty years to move three miles away. Twenty years in boxes. Was it a mid-life crisis or a good idea?

As I was packing box No. 32, Hannah asked, "Tell me again why we're doing this, Mommy?"

It seemed like a good idea at the time.

The new house is bigger, in a quieter place, on higher ground, far from the maddening crowd, far from the store, the newspaper box, the cafe, the mailbox, the traffic: in short, far from everything except damn beautiful nature.

As soon as we brought our first belongings to the new house, a neighbor arrived to tell us which tree to remove. Another handsome couple politely asked if their nude sunbathing would bother our children. Out back, we heard a distant guitar. A man was doing nude t'ai chi as his girlfriend played "Guantanamara."

Welcome to California.

We are drained. We have run the gauntlet of real estate torture. We have been buyers and sellers. We have visited title companies and loan officers and placed our initials next to an endless line of X's that stand for: OK, take all my money.

We have supposedly moved up, yet I know I haven't

packed up my troubles in my old kit bag. I've just moved my old kit bag to a new set of troubles. I'm still the same miserable person I always was.

Although we've moved up and ought to be in home-owner heaven, the list of things we could do to make the place better grows with each person who checks it out. We could paint the kitchen. We could refinish the floors. We could landscape the yard. (One landscaper told me it's the worst yard he's ever seen, and he wouldn't touch it for less than twenty-five grand!) We could get rugs. We could get rattan furniture. We could get a microwave. We should get a roof.

Only problem is we just spent our wad and quadrupled our mortgage payments.

Which brings me back to what the kid said when she said the darnedest thing: Why are we doing this?

Of course, we're doing it for the children. And they hate us for it. "I want to go home," they keep saying.

"When are we going to go to our *real* house?" asks Hannah. And I know what she means. Every night I wake up at 3:00 A.M. and think: This is a very nice place, but it's time to go home.

No, we really did it to get *away* from the children. We've got teenagers coming. We've got to take cover. The house has "good separation," as they say in Real-estatespeak.

We did it because the trouble with staying in one place too long is that you notice all the changes and they piss you off. More traffic. More cars. Parking regulations that turned our once sleepy block into a parking lot. We moved to get a parking place.

One couple in the old neighborhood had decided to help the homeless. They rented out their old, broken-down car, which was parked on the block, to a man who talks to trees. He also urinates on houses.

I suppose some people would say it's part of my growing conservatism that I wanted to protect my children from him.

The day before we moved, another street crazy tried to kick my twelve-year-old daughter as she walked around him. He screamed curses at her. She looked at me with big, innocent eyes and asked, "What did he call me?"

I had thought I would die in the old house. It was the first single-family house I ever lived in. It was the American dream. To live in a place with an upstairs and a downstairs and a wonderful little yard and an attic and a tree house and the oak hall tree that we found and refinished and mounted in the hall. The new owner came in with her personal carpenter and looked at our hall tree and said, "We'll yank that out first thing."

Then she's going to go over the walls "with a blowtorch" and really fix the place up. Then she's going to yank out my new black and white tile kitchen floor—my dream kitchen floor!

Keeping buyers and sellers apart—this is why God invented real estate people.

I loved that house. Home and mother. Home and mother. I have no mother, and now I have no home. Just a large furnished debt.

I think of my late mother making the steerage journey from Suwalk, Poland, to America. America. Now, I come by Datsun wagon to the hills of California only to suffer nature-shock. It's too pretty around here.

I try to make myself at home. I grab a Sierra Nevada Pale Ale and put Curtis Mayfield on my tape machine. He keeps singing, "It's all right to have a good time." I try to convince myself it's true.

We moved to be good Americans. We did it because it is our God-given duty to acquire more debt. We did it because the average American moves eleven times in a lifetime. I've moved nine. That gives me two more turns before the Big Broker takes me to that shtetl in the sky.

Where Has All the Gone World Gone?

Whither goest thou, man? I mean, what ever happened to all the beatniks?

I don't mean Allen Ginsberg or Jack Kerouac or Lawrence Ferlinghetti—your celebrity beatniks. I'm talking about the rank and file, the Ozzie and Harriet beatnik, the folks who stuck it out through all those poetry readings. Who now from L.A. mansions or Philadelphia townhomes or St. Louis one-window hotel rooms, or from most holy, holy Terre Haute, roam the angry streets at dawn looking for Geritol.

I know what happened to the hippies. Every time I attend the opening party for a new restaurant or computer firm or real estate office, I have the same fantasy:

I walk into a roomful of people chatting politely while stuffing themselves with warm goat cheese and swilling down their sauvignon blanc—men with stylish crew cuts, skinny neckties and suspenders and loose gray jackets with sleeves pushed up to the elbows; women in short, tight black skirts and black high heels and oversized sweaters with shoulder pads and loose gray jackets with sleeves pushed up to the elbows. Then I try to picture them as they would have looked fifteen years ago—half naked, hair to the waist, barefoot, Indian bedspread clothes, dancing wildly creative frugs at a Free Huey fund-raiser.

Some say the hippies were justs beatniks with more drugs, beatniks who said, "Oooh. Wow. The colors . . ." but it was different. The hippies were a mass phenomenon. Hippies had millions of rock 'n' roll records to tell them how to be hippies. Every town and village in America had hippies. But beatniks were a few isolated souls who listened to distant drummers in dim-lit little Birdlands of the heart.

Yeah.

When I was a teenager in Chicago, sometimes we'd "go beat." That meant we'd dress up in black turtlenecks and wear lots of eye makeup and white lipstick and go down to a place called Bug House Square, where crazy people talked about free love and socialism and the Negroes.

Then we would try to get into a nightclub called The College of Complexes, where I believe actual Negroes played jazz while white kids sat with their eyes closed, pounding on the tables. I don't know. I never got in. The owner never bought our phony ID or our phony act.

At fifteen, I got an after-school job selling magazine subscriptions on the phone. Anything to get out of the house. I would sit there in the office reading *On the Road*, in between phoning people and saying "Congratulations! You have just won a free year of *Reader's Digest*, *Look* and *Collier's*. Now all you have to do is . . ."

And I would dream of escaping Eisenhower's America and running away with the beatniks and being a nonconformist. Mostly, I would dream about Sonny Becker. He lived down the block and did nothing all day. He wore a black leather jacket. You could hear jazz echoing from his room late at night. He was friends with the Negroes. My big sister, Myrna, told me he once offered her some "tea," and not the kind you drink, either.

Yes, someday Sonny would take me away in a beat-up old convertible, and we would write haiku and play bongos while the dark night of America rolled by the windows. But Sonny's family moved uptown and Kennedy became president, and I went to college and started writing sonnets and villanelles and thought free verse was "sloppy."

So, Sonny, man, if you're listening, what the hell ever happened to you? Did you end up in San Francisco in beatnik heaven or did you get a job?

Judy, It Was Not for Naught that We Did Nothing

Somewhere out there in Ohio, Judy Cohen O'Brien is still worried about a bad rep. So worried that she called Helena Feldman Erlich in Los Angeles for a consult. And this is the only way I can tell her: Relax, Judy, it wasn't you.

Judy's been worried about her reputation for twenty-five years, since she graduated from my high school in Chicago. To me, she'll always be a cool "older" girl—older than me—with a brush cut and a bucket bag.

But apparently she's also an Ohio housewife whose deepest fears were triggered when she got hold of a book I wrote several years ago. The first story in the book described what life was like for adolescent girls in the bad old days before the birth control pill. It was about the one girl who broke the rules.

After reading the book, Judy sent a letter to me via Ten Speed Press, the publisher. "It was with absolute horror that I turned to the first story, 'High School Nympho,'" wrote Cohen O'Brien. "Did she have a brush cut? Did she always carry a big purse? Would she be described as learning how to smoke at age thirteen at Harry's? Was she me?"

There were several funny things about this letter. One was that I had a brush cut, carried a big purse and learned to smoke at age thirteen at Harry's school store. So that killed the fantasy of my own uniqueness.

The other funny thing was how the letter punctured my theory of the high school nympho (HSN). Judy offered the names of several potential nymphos from our past. I thought each school was issued just one.

See, back then most of us were willing to go "some of the way" but lived in terror of the complications of taking things to the limit. My story, in addition to describing the seemingly charmed life of our HSN, also described the tragic life of the Girl Who Got Pregnant.

Judy wanted to set the record straight. She explained that her best friend, Helena Feldman (now Erlich), "kept me virginal by swearing she wasn't doing anything—and I didn't want to be the one they talked about."

Then she offered the names of two girls who *could* have been the HSN. Interestingly, neither candidate was the girl I had in mind, the one about whom everyone said: She *had* to have it.

Meanwhile, Judy and Helena are worried that I might have meant *them*, and I have no way to relieve their anxiety. "Our breaths are bated for your answer," Judy wrote.

But the final funny thing is that Ten Speed Press lost the envelope with the return address, and all I have is Judy's description of her Ohio town as "like being at a giant casting call for *Deliverance*."

So, Mrs. O'Brien of Deliverance, Ohio, here's the whole story. While you were trying to go no further than Helena (who was gorgeous and had half the boys in the school running after her), I was trying to go no further than my best friend, Penny (who wasn't even dating). I fell in love my junior year with a boy who finally left me because I wouldn't "prove" my love. He was a chemist and demanded proof. All I ever asked of him was a hypothesis.

After we split up, I sat home and cried every night for

six months because I was heartbroken. But I could never forget the Girl Who Got Pregnant. You knew exactly who *she* was, Judy, as you said in your letter. Who could forget what happened to her? Remember how she was kicked off the cheerleading squad and then kicked out of school? Remember how everyone stopped talking to her? Do you remember people wiping off the desk after she sat there?

The "nympho," by contrast, was popular, happy and cheerful. What was behind her Gioconda smile? Could it have been—condoms?

No, Judy, it wasn't you, and it wasn't Helena, and it wasn't me.

I guess there must be a lot of fearful readers out there. So, as a public service, will the real high school nympho please stand up and tell us your story?

Better yet, maybe it's time for a high school nympho reunion. We'll probably need Wrigley Field.

What Makes Old Frank, Dean and Sammy Run?

If your last concert was a Grateful Dead show, you immediately noticed the absence of tie-dye at the Ratpack Reunion. You also noticed the motionless audience glued to their seats like a painted backdrop. Not a bootie shook.

Unlike most of the women there, I wasn't in the audience because I loved Frank. To me he was like that boozy old uncle you had to flirt with because it was too cruel not to.

I was of that generation that gladly spurned Frank for Elvis. But now I wanted him and Dean and Sammy to pinch my cheek and call me "kiddo" one more time. Even if they'd never be hip, let them try to prove they were still hep. Let them show that they could still cut the musical mustard.

Long live my hairy-eared uncles from the old countries of New York and New Jersey and Chicago. This was the Do Not Go Gentle into That Good Night tour.

It was in its own way a solemn night—a night of respect for Frank, support for alcohol-free Sammy and prayer for the tragic clown, Dean Martin.

It was a night of fighting loss—Frank's alleged loss of his voice (you coulda fooled me); Sammy's loss of his hip (recently surgically replaced); but most of all Dean's loss of his son, who died on March 21, 1987, in a plane crash.

No one has said this, but obviously underwriting the tour are some friends trying to tell a pal, "Pick yourself up and get back in the race."

In the wings, a nurse from the Haight-Ashbury Free Clinic waited—not to treat acid freakouts but to administer nitroglycerin in case the stars developed angina. She worried, too, about how much longer the lines of aging bobby-soxers outside the women's rooms were going to get. "Wait till their diuretic starts working," she said.

With her was a local throat specialist who, she explained, had been called in at the last minute because "they're worried about Frank's voice." The throat guy, Dr. Andrew Moyce of Oakland, looked nervous as he envisioned standing over the Chairman's tonsils while some pug pointed a machine gun at his head and said, "Fix him up, Doc."

My friend Dobby, who came with me, likes to characterize a social occasion in terms of what jokes are appropriate. "Don't make Mafia jokes," he kept saying. "Show respect for Frank."

The crowds of fake Mafia and real bimbos and fake fur and polyester and black, shiny, pointed loafers and silver spike heels giggled nervously as Dean came out. The joking about booze was thin. The man could barely maintain. Don't fall, Dean, we prayed.

Standing there with the painted smile was Pagliacci, singing, "Bring my baby back to me." The man had lost his baby, not his voice. We shared his grief as he wiped off the sweat and the tears, and, oh so slowly, climbed from the stage.

Then Sammy jumped in, trying not to look and sound too much like Jerry Lewis. Going "Ch-kong, ch-kong" with his soul brother on the drums, he swung that new hip—refined through the pain of countless physical-therapy sessions—to a triumph this night. He was the Michael Jackson of his time, another freak saved by undeniable talent.

When Frank came out, it was as if Bing Crosby, Billie Holiday, Mayor Daley and Julius Caesar had all come back to life. *He* made the Mafia jokes. He set the rhythm. He concentrated to hit the high notes. He felt the songs so deeply, you really wanted to cry.

When the pack came out for the finale, they didn't sing "Friendship," but they did do "Side by Side." As Dino stumbled through, his pals picked up the slack. At no time did Sammy grab Frank and say, "This man, ladies and gentlemen—I love this man." But it was obvious.

And you started to wonder what the future holds. Hard to imagine Bruce Springsteen doing Geritol and prune-juice jokes. Or Bob Dylan being subjected to you-don't-look-Jewish jokes, as Sammy was. Or Keith Richards forcing Mick Jagger back on the road when the road gets rougher and lonelier and tougher.

With my own parents long gone, I came to cheer Uncle Dean and Uncle Sammy and Uncle Frank and ask them, one more time: Sing those sad songs for me.

Chicago's a Ghost Town

I wasn't planning to visit the folks this year. I was on a business trip. Yet as soon as I got in the airspace above Chicago, I heard my father's voice. He was telling the same old story, the story he told a thousand times. The story of how he started down the road of fame and fortune and misfortune.

"We had the parks, we had White City, we had Navy Pier," I heard him saying as my plane circled the town with streets so straight you'd think a giant ruler had marked out the prairie.

My father died here almost a quarter-century ago while I was still in my teens, so long ago he seems like a movie to me. I left Chicago shortly after he died, wanting never to return again.

Now I like to come home because, in fact, it's the only place I can still hear my father. It took me years to make peace with this town, years to make peace with my parents, longer still to make peace with their deaths. Now it's all buried here in Chicago—that toddlin' town.

The story my father told over and over again was how as a young man hanging out at Puddies, the local pool hall, he met Jimmy McGrat, described as "the Irish boss of Madison Street." At night, he said, he would "put long pants over my short and go out cabareting with Jimmy." At some point, he quit school and went to work as Jimmy's "right-hand man." He would have been about fifteen.

I picture him like a young ghetto hustler today, working for some big crack king, living in style, taking crazy risks with his life, thinking work was for "chumps."

He spent the Roaring Twenties with Jimmy. I don't know if he packed a piece or just carried around bags of cash for the man. I'm not even sure what he meant by "we had the parks, we had White City, we had Navy Pier." I think they were all places where games were played and food was sold. I assume it meant they controlled these operations or got paid protection money by the proprietors.

At some time my father started wearing silk shirts and calling himself the "Silk Shirt Kid," and he used that name when he was old and fat and bald and reminiscing. He talked about "a broad with two Russian wolfhounds," who would have been my mother, I guess, if things had worked out.

Things went badly for Jimmy. And as he fell, so did the Silk Shirt Kid.

According to the legend, "Jimmy McGrat fell in love with a burlesque queen. He bought the Columbia Burlesque wheel to make her a star." But Silky knew better. "I told him, 'Jimmy, burlesque is going out, and musicals is coming in.' But he was in love. He wouldn't listen. Two years later—he went bust."

"What happened to Jimmy, Daddy?" I would ask over and over again, although I knew the story always had the same tragic end.

"We bought him a little restaurant at the train station," Silky would say. "But here's a guy used to spending a G a day. Now he was making that much maybe in a month. So within a year—he went under."

In time I learned the key to this story. Going bust

referred to your money. But going under referred to your life.

Eventually, the Silk Shirt Kid went legit. He got married, had kids, worked at running some movie theaters. To the day he died, he missed the risky days of his youth, regretting that he could not have both high times and peace of mind. As a result of regretting, he had neither.

I like being a Californian. I like living in a place where I have no history, no memories, no roots beyond the ones I've planted myself. So there is a dreamlike feeling when I'm back in my hometown. Walking along Lake Michigan at 8:00 A.M., I feel more at home than near San Francisco Bay, where I've lived most of my life.

I never hear my father's voice in San Francisco, the new world. It's something I left behind, as he left his father's voice back in Europe.

Lake Michigan is not the Pacific Ocean, of course, but it's still a great lake. The ornate brick buildings lining its shore did not have to withstand a major earthquake. And the humidity sits on your shoulders worse than gravity. I would never leave California to live here, but it is my home. It's the place my father helped build before he went under. He'll always be here.

Out on the lake I see two buildings at what they call Navy Pier. Lake Michigan was really something in the old days. At one time, we had the parks, we had White City, we had Navy Pier. . . .

(*continued from page* 6)

The San Francisco Chronicle:

"Born with a Silver Popcorn Box"; "The Gods Must Be Nasty"; "Pianotherapy"; "What If They Had a Meeting and Artists Came?"; "Kind of a Rambo-Hegel Sort of Thing"; "A Writer's Guide to Editorial Fauna"; "Money Can't Buy You Acreage"; "The Pauline Kael of Porn"; "Coming of Age with the Niners"; "Columnist Is a Tramp"; "Life Is Short, but Art Can Take All Night"; " 'Biff,' a Celebrity Drug Abuser"; "Born-Again Hetero"; "A Man's Home Is His Restaurant"; "Where Have All the G Spots Gone?"; "Bathroom Lib"; "Midway Through the Battle of Mid-life"; "Cher Gives Us a Nose Job"; "Life's Little Cardless Moments"; "Finding That Special Psychotherapeutic Someone"; "I Saw London, I Saw France"; "Sex So Safe You'll Never Want It Again"; "Mondo Bizarro Scientifique"; "The Temple of Lifestyle"; "Little Myth Female"; "Dolphin Show at the L.A. Dude Ranch"; "The Little Shop of Electrodes"; "Go to the Head of the Middle Class"; "Valley of the Silicone Dolls"; "Help for the Chronically Stressless"; "Through the Looking Class, Darkly"; "My Life as a Piece of Data"; "Channeling for Dollars"; "Guess Who's Coming to Passover Dinner"; "A Sibling Reverie"; "The Family That Shabooms Together"; "When Grandma Was a Transvestite"; "Where Have You Gone, Joe Geronimo?"; "Stress Reduction for Seven-Year-Olds"; "Art Is Dog Spelled Backwards"; "You Can't Teach an Old Moon New Tricks"; "The Swinging Single Life with Kids"; "Rebel with a Tapered Cause"; "Tough Guys Don't Squirm in the Jewelry Store"; "The Aging Dork and Her She-Monster"; "I'm the Number on Dustin Hoffman's Dashboard"; "The Bicoastal Network Hot-Line Trend"; "Phone Zombie Torments College Prof"; "The Day I Drove the Disk Drive Down"; "Read My Beeps"; "VCR Illiteracy: A National Scandal"; "Candi's Hang-up"; "Whoever You Are, I Can't Get You Out of My Mind"; "Nothing but a WASP"; "Women's Glib—All About Al"; "I Gave My Love a Lawn Mower"; "What Makes Seth Cool?"; "My Life as a Man"; "The Unimportance of Being Ken"; "Time After Time . . . A Table for Two"; "These Are a Few of My Favorite Years"; "The Alumni News: Class Notes"; "Joe Variable Rate, Meet Mary Fixed"; "The Moment When History Began"; "These Foolish Things Remind Me of You"; "Are We in California Yet, Mommy?"; "Where Has All the Gone World Gone?"; "Judy, It Was Not for Naught that We Did Nothing"; "What Makes Old Frank, Dean and Sammy Run?"; "Chicago's a Ghost Town"